cheat your way to gourmet eating

carolyn humphries

foulsham

LONDON • NEW YORK • TORONTO • SYDNEY

foulsham

The Publishing House, Bennetts Close, Cippenham,
Slough, Berkshire, SL1 5AP, England

ISBN 0-572-03069-X

Cover and inside photographs by Phil Wilkins

Home economist Amanda Phipps

A CIP record for this book is available from the British Library

Printed in Great Britain by St Edmundsbury Press, Bury St Edmunds, Suffolk

Contents

Introduction

Are you, like most of us, too busy to cook but tired of cook-chill meals, bored with takeaways and fed-up with frozen microwave menus? Do you worry that your diet is downright unhealthy and in need of a boost? If your answers are yes, the solutions are right here. Clever, classy cheating that not only makes huge short cuts on effort but also saves so much time you'll be able to do all the things you used to do while your ready meals were heating up! Not only that, you'll use a brilliant combination of fresh, nutritious ingredients alongside the best convenience foods, so your diet will be much improved.

Everyone will be hugely impressed with your new-found culinary genius too, because most of them will be equally uninspired by supermarket suppers and these dishes will look as if you've slaved over a hot stove for hours. Little will they know they were thrown together in minutes! Some serve four and others six but most can be divided or multiplied, if necessary, to feed as many or as few as you need them to. Dip into this book for everything from a quick snack to a complete three-course dinner. From now on you'll have time to cook and chill out, rather than endure the cook-chill phenomenon.

Basic food hygiene

A hygienic cook is a healthy cook – so please bear the following in mind when you're preparing food.

- Always wash your hands before preparing food.

- Always wash and dry fresh produce before use.

- Don't lick your fingers.

- Don't keep tasting and stirring with the same spoon. Use a clean spoon every time you taste the food.

- Don't put raw and cooked meat on the same shelf in the fridge. Store raw meat on the bottom shelf, so its juices can't drip over other foods. Keep all perishable foods wrapped separately. Don't overfill the fridge or it will become too warm.

- Never use a cloth to wipe down a chopping board you have been using for cutting meat, for instance, then use the same one to wipe down your work surfaces – you will simply spread germs. Always wash your cloth well between uses in hot, soapy water and, ideally, use an anti-bacterial kitchen cleaner on all surfaces too.

- Always transfer leftovers to a clean container and cover with a lid, clingfilm (plastic wrap) or foil. Leave until completely cold, then store in the fridge. Never put any warm food in the fridge and always cool food as quickly as possible – don't leave it lying around all day!

- When reheating food, always make sure it is piping hot throughout, never just lukewarm. To test made-up dishes, such as lasagne or a pie, insert a knife down through the centre. Leave for 5 seconds and remove. The blade should feel extremely hot. If it isn't, heat the dish for a little longer.

- Don't re-freeze foods that have defrosted unless you cook them first. Never reheat previously cooked food more than once.

Storecupboard specialities

A well-stocked kitchen will mean you can cook any of the recipes whenever you feel like it. Obviously this is just a guide that you can tailor to your own requirements.

Packets and jars

- baking powder
- bicarbonate of soda (baking soda)
- bulgar (cracked wheat)
- caviare – avruga or lumpfish roe
- chocolate spread
- cocoa (unsweetened chocolate) powder
- cornflour (cornstarch)
- couscous
- cranberry sauce
- dried fruits – apricots, mixed (fruit cake mix), raisins, sultanas (golden raisins)
- dried milk powder (non-fat dry milk)
- dried minced onion
- flour – plain (all-purpose), self-raising (rising), wholemeal
- garlic purée (paste) in a tube or jar – if you can't be bothered to crush the cloves. Use about 5 ml/1 tsp in place of one large garlic clove or to taste
- golden (light corn) syrup
- herbs: dried – basil, bay leaves, bouquet garni sachets, chives, mint, mixed, oregano, parsley, sage, thyme
- herbs: jars, minced – coriander (cilantro), garden mint, lemon grass, parsley
- honey – clear is best for cooking
- horseradish relish
- instant coffee
- instant drinking (sweetened) chocolate powder (one you just add boiling water to)
- jelly (jello)

- lemon curd
- lemon/lime juice – a bottle of each will keep in the fridge for ages
- marmalade and other conserves
- Marmite or other yeast extract
- marshmallows
- mayonnaise
- mustard – Dijon, made English, wholegrain
- nuts – ground almonds, flaked (slivered) almonds, cashews, peanuts, pine, walnuts
- oils – corn or groundnut (peanut), sunflower, olive, speciality oils such as sesame and walnut for flavouring
- olives
- passata (sieved tomatoes)
- pasta – lasagne sheets, macaroni and/or other shapes, spaghetti, stuffed tortellini
- pepper – black peppercorns in a mill, ground white
- pesto
- pickled quails' eggs
- redcurrant jelly (clear conserve)
- rice – long-grain, microwave, mushroom risotto and other savoury packets, round-grain (pudding), wild
- salt – celery, garlic, onion, plain
- sauces for cooking such as Bolognese, curry, hoi sin, oyster, teryiaki, tomato and basil
- seeds – caraway, poppy, sesame, sunflower
- spices – cayenne, chilli powder, Chinese five-spice, cinnamon, cloves, coriander (cilantro), cumin, curry powder, mixed (apple pie), nutmeg, sweet paprika, pimentón, turmeric
- stock cubes – beef, chicken, vegetable
- sugar – dark brown, light brown, caster (superfine), granulated, icing (confectioners')

- table sauces – barbecue, brown, ketchup (catsup), soy, Tabasco, Worcestershire. Chilli and Worcestershire and tomato table sauces are great too
- tapenade
- tomato purée (paste)
- vinegar – balsamic, malt, red or white wine or cider

Canny cans

- baby clams
- Chinese mixed vegetables
- coconut milk
- condensed soups – celery, mushroom, tomato (ideal for sauces)
- crab – white meat, dressed
- custard
- evaporated milk
- fruit – apricots, grapefruit, melon balls, mixed berries, peaches, pears, pineapple, raspberries
- mushrooms – creamed, sliced, whole button
- pulses – borlotti, cannellini, flageolet, haricot (navy), red kidney and soya beans, chick peas (garbanzos), lentils, mixed pulses
- salmon
- smoked oysters
- steak – minced, stewed
- sweetcorn (corn)
- tomatoes – chopped are quickest
- tuna (check the label for 'dolphin friendly')
- vegetables – asparagus, carrots, French (green) beans, peas, pimientos, potatoes (useful for some of the recipes and for quick accompaniments)

Perishables

- breads – including ciabatta, naan, pittas, rolls, tortillas, etc. Store in the freezer until required
- butter and/or margarine or other spread
- cheese – blue, Camembert, Cheddar, goats', medium-fat soft, Mozarella, Parmesan
- cream – double (heavy), single (light)
- crème fraîche
- eggs (preferably free-range) – medium, large
- herbs, frozen chopped – coriander (cilantro), mint, parsley
- meats – frozen chicken breasts and livers, minced (ground) beef and lamb, diced lamb and pork, lamb and pork chops and fillet, steaks
- milk – keep a carton in the freezer so you won't run out but it takes ages to thaw and needs a good shake once defrosted
- pastry (paste) – frozen filo, puff and shortcrust (basic pie crust)
- seafood – frozen cod, plaice, mixed, prawns
- vegetables – frozen, including chips (fries), hash browns, peas, potato wedges, spinach
- yoghurt – plain

Basic fresh vegetables

Some other vegetables, like green (French) beans, courgettes, (bell) peppers and aubergines (eggplants), keep well; others, such as greens and brassicas, are best bought as you need them and used within a few days.

- carrots
- garlic
- herbs in pots – basil, parsley, etc.
- mushrooms
- onions
- potatoes – old and new
- salad stuffs – cucumber, lettuce, tomatoes etc.

Notes on the recipes

- All ingredients are given in imperial, metric and American measures. Follow one set only in a recipe. American terms are given in brackets.

- Ingredients are listed in the order in which they are used.

- All spoon measures are level: 1 tsp = 5 ml; 1 tbsp = 15 ml.

- Eggs are medium unless otherwise stated.

- Always wash, peel, core and seed, if necessary, fresh produce before use.

- Seasoning and the use of strongly flavoured ingredients such as garlic or chillies is very much a matter of personal taste. Taste the food as you cook and adjust to suit your own palate.

- Fresh herbs are great for garnishing and adding flavour. Pots of them are available in all good supermarkets. Keep a few of your favourites ones on the windowsill and water regularly. Jars of ready-prepared herbs, such as coriander (cilantro) and lemon grass, and frozen herbs – chopped parsley in particular – are also very useful. I use a mixture of these and dried ones in the recipes. Don't substitute dried when fresh are called for; there is always a good reason why I've used them!

- All can and packet sizes are approximate as they vary from brand to brand. For example, if I call for a 400 g/14 oz/ large can of tomatoes and yours is a 397 g can – that's fine.

- Cooking times are approximate and should be used as a guide only. Always check food is piping hot and cooked through before serving.

- Always preheat the oven and cook on the shelf just above the centre unless otherwise stated. Fan ovens do not need preheating and the positioning is not so crucial.

- Many recipes call for cream or crème fraîche. You must use a full-fat variety if the dish is boiled after it is added, as low-fat creams will curdle. You may substitute low-fat varieties for cold dishes, garnishes or decorations or if it is stirred into a hot dish at the last minute without boiling.

9

starters

It's great if friends turn up unexpectedly and you can knock up
a little starter without turning a hair. And, even if you want
something really special, with a well-stocked larder, fridge and
freezer you can create a whole repertoire using the wonderful
cheats in this chapter. So get your guests' taste buds tingling
and make something that will truly impress them. What's more,
the recipes are so easy you'll have plenty of time to enjoy your
pre-dinner drinks and chit chat with them!

Sautéed chicken livers with cumin-spiced borlotti beans

This delicious dish is made up of little mounds of delicately spiced borlotti beans,
topped with chicken livers lightly sautéed in butter and port to add richness and
depth. It also makes a tasty lunch dish served with a salad and crusty bread.
You can use chick peas instead of the beans if you prefer.

SERVES 6

200 g/7 oz frozen chicken livers, thawed

30 ml/2 tbsp olive oil, plus extra for drizzling

1 onion, very finely chopped

1 small garlic clove, crushed, or 2.5 ml/½ tsp garlic purée (paste)

15 ml/1 tbsp ground cumin

5 ml/1 tsp sweet paprika, plus extra for dusting

2 x 425 g/15 oz/large cans of borlotti beans, drained, rinsed and drained again

Salt and freshly ground black pepper

A good pinch of caster (superfine) sugar

2.5 ml/½ tsp bottled lemon juice

15 g/½ oz/1 tbsp butter

60 ml/4 tbsp port

A little chopped fresh parsley, to garnish

1 Trim the chicken livers and cut into bite-sized pieces.

2 Heat half the olive oil in a saucepan. Add the onion and stir over a gentle heat for about 3 minutes until soft but not brown.

3 Add the garlic, cumin and paprika and cook, stirring, for 30 seconds.

4 Add the beans and stir to coat. Season well with salt and pepper to taste and the sugar and lemon juice. Heat through.

5 In a separate pan, heat the remaining oil and the butter. Add the chicken livers and cook, stirring, for 2 minutes until lightly browned but still soft and pink in the centre.

6 Add the port and a little salt and pepper and simmer for a further 2–3 minutes, stirring all the time, until most of the liquid has evaporated.

7 Spoon a sixth of the bean mixture into a ramekin dish (custard cup) and press down. Turn out on to a small warm serving plate. Repeat with the remaining beans. Spoon the chicken livers and their juices on top.

8 Sprinkle a little chopped parsley on top of each. Drizzle a little olive oil round the edge of each plate and dust with a little paprika. Serve straight away.

Thai-style crispy seafood sticks

Juicy, tender seafood sticks, flavoured with strips of spring onion and a little crushed lemon grass are here wrapped in golden filo pastry and served with a sweet chilli dipping sauce. You can buy prawns treated in this way but they are very expensive. This version is incredibly economical and takes no time to prepare.

SERVES 6

1 bunch of spring onions (scallions)

3 sheets of filo pastry (paste)

Sunflower oil

30 ml/2 tbsp lemon grass paste from a jar

24 seafood sticks

Oil for deep-frying

1 bottle of sweet chilli dipping sauce

1 Take six of the spring onions and either cut them in diagonal slices for garnish or make spring onion flowers, if you want to be really impressive!. To do this, trim off the roots and trim the green part to leave the onions about 7.5 cm/3 in long. Using a sharp knife, make several cuts, about 2.5 cm/1 in long, in both ends of each onion. Place the onions in a bowl of cold water and chill to open out.

2 Trim the ends off the remaining onions and cut into very thin strips about the same length as the seafood sticks.

3 Lay a sheet of filo pastry on a board, keeping the remaining two covered with clingfilm (plastic wrap) or a damp cloth to prevent drying out. Brush with a little oil. Cut it in half lengthways, then cut each half into four smaller rectangles.

4 Spread the lemon grass sparingly over the centre of each rectangle. Take a third of the spring onion strips and lay an equal amount diagonally on each of the eight rectangles. Top each with a seafood stick, also diagonally. Fold in the ends, then roll up from one point of the rectangle to form parcels. Repeat with the remaining ingredients.

5 Heat the oil for deep-frying to 190°C/375°F or until a cube of day-old bread browns in 30 seconds. Deep-fry the parcels in batches for about 3 minutes until golden brown, turning once. Drain on kitchen paper (paper towels) and keep warm while cooking the remainder.

6 Arrange on a platter with a bowl of chilli dipping sauce in the centre. Drain the spring onion flowers, if using, and arrange around for garnish or scatter the reserved slices over.

Prawns and artichoke hearts with caviare

*Soft, almost creamy-textured artichoke hearts mingled with plump, succulent prawns
in a delicate herb-flavoured marinade are topped with cool crème fraîche and opulent
caviare. The whole thing looks and tastes terrific but takes no more than a few
minutes to put together!*

SERVES 6

2 x 425 g/15 oz/large cans of artichoke
hearts, drained and quartered

225 g/8 oz frozen cooked, peeled
prawns (shrimp), thawed

45 ml/3 tbsp olive oil

15 ml/1 tbsp bottled lemon juice

Salt and freshly ground black pepper

10 ml/2 tsp snipped fresh or
5 ml/1 tsp dried chives

15 ml/1 tbsp chopped fresh parsley

90 ml/6 tbsp crème fraîche

1 x 50 g/2 oz/small jar of avruga caviare
or Danish lumpfish roe

TO SERVE
Very thin brown bread and butter or
Melba Toast (see page 127)

1 Dry the artichokes on kitchen paper (paper towels) and place in a bowl. Dry the prawns on kitchen paper and add to the artichokes.

2 Whisk the oil, lemon juice, a pinch of salt and a good grinding of pepper with the chives and parsley. Pour over the artichokes and prawns and toss gently with your hands to coat completely. Cover and chill for 1 hour to allow the flavours to develop if time.

3 Spoon the mixture into six wine goblets or small serving bowls. Top each with 15 ml/1 tbsp of the crème fraîche, then some caviare. Serve with very thin brown bread and butter or Melba Toast.

Pear and mortadella crustades

For this dish, crisp, buttery bread cases are filled with tender mortadella and sweet pears bathed in a tangy blue cheese mayonnaise. If you are in a real hurry, forget the bread cases and just serve the pears laid in the centre of large slices of mortadella with a creamy blue cheese dressing spooned over the top.

SERVES 6

6 slices of brown bread from a cut loaf, crusts removed

Butter

150 ml/¼ pt/⅔ cup bottled blue cheese dressing

30 ml/2 tbsp single (light) cream

Freshly ground black pepper

6 slices of mortadella

6 canned pear halves

Paprika and a few wild rocket leaves, to garnish

1 Spread the bread on both sides with butter. Press into six ramekin dishes (custard cups) or sections of a large muffin tin (pan). Bake in a preheated oven at 190°C/375°F/gas 5/fan oven 170°C for about 25 minutes until golden and crisp. Leave to cool, then remove from the ramekins or tin.

2 Mix the dressing with the cream and season with pepper.

3 Line the bread cases with the slices of mortadella. Dry the pear halves on kitchen paper (paper towels), then lay one rounded-side up in each case. Spoon the dressing over.

4 Transfer the bread cases to small serving plates. Dust the tops with a little paprika and arrange a few wild rocket leaves to one side.

Chicken satay sticks with crispy seaweed

Sometimes it's all about presentation. Here is everybody's favourite little chicken kebabs nestling on a bed of crispy greens with a little bowl of spicy peanut sauce for dipping – perfect. The sauce uses all storecupboard standbys but you can use bought ready-made peanut sauce if you prefer.

SERVES 6

120 ml/4 fl oz/½ cup water

15 ml/1 tbsp dried chives

15 ml/1 tbsp dried minced onion

225 g/8 oz/1 cup smooth peanut butter

15 ml/1 tbsp clear honey

30 ml/2 tbsp soy sauce

A few drops of Tabasco sauce

36 ready-cooked chicken satay sticks

2 x 55g/2¼ oz packs of crispy seaweed

1 Put the water, chives and onion in a small saucepan. Bring to the boil, turn down the heat and simmer for 1 minute. Blend in the peanut butter, honey and soy sauce and stir until smooth. Remove from the heat. Add a few drops of Tabasco sauce to taste.

2 When nearly ready to serve, heat the chicken satay sticks and seaweed according to the packet instructions. Reheat the sauce.

3 Spoon the sauce into six small ramekin dishes (custard cups). Place on one side of warm serving plates and spoon the seaweed alongside. Arrange the satay sticks attractively on top and serve.

Quails' egg and pâté tartlets

A sumptuous mixture of pâté, tiny eggs and olives nestling in meltingly short pastry cases, this makes a very sophisticated starter. If you want to cook fresh quails' eggs, put them in water, bring to the boil and cook for 3 minutes only. Drain and plunge immediately into cold water to prevent further cooking, then shell when cold.

SERVES 6

½ chicken stock cube

150 ml/¼ pt/⅔ cup boiling water

10 ml/2 tsp powdered gelatine

225 g/8 oz frozen shortcrust pastry (basic pie crust), thawed

75 g/3 oz smooth liver pâté

75 g/3 oz/⅓ cup medium-fat soft cheese

15 ml/1 tbsp brandy

15 ml/1 tbsp milk

Salt and freshly ground black pepper

6 quails' eggs in brine or vinegar, drained

6 black stoned (pitted) olives, halved

6 green stoned olives, halved

A few fresh chive stalks or coriander (cilantro) sprigs, to garnish

1 Stir the stock cube into the boiling water until dissolved. Stir in the gelatine until completely dissolved. Leave to cool, then chill until the consistency of egg white.

2 Meanwhile, roll out the pastry (paste) and use to line six individual flan rings set on a baking (cookie) sheet or in flan dishes.

3 Prick the bases with a fork, then fill with crumpled foil. Bake in a preheated oven at 200°C/400°F/gas 6/fan oven 180°C for 10 minutes. Remove the foil and return to the oven for 5 minutes to dry out. Leave to cool.

4 Beat the pâté with the cheese, brandy and milk to form a soft consistency that still holds its shape. Season to taste. Spoon into the cases and level the surfaces.

5 Dry the eggs on kitchen paper (paper towels). Place one in the centre of each flan and two halves of black and two halves of green olive round each egg.

6 Spoon the jellied stock over each flan, then chill.

7 To serve, remove the flan rings if necessary. Place the flans on serving plates, lay a few chive stalks or a long sprig of coriander to one side of each plate and serve.

Grilled goats' cheese with cranberry and walnut dressing

This is a combination of ever-popular flavours that creates a very easy but impressive starter worthy of your local bistro. The dressing takes about a minute to whisk together (most of it is ready-made after all!) and the cheese only a few minutes to melt slightly under the grill.

SERVES 6

1 x 125 g/4½ oz/small packet of mixed salad leaves

50 g/2 oz/½ cup walnuts, roughly chopped

60 ml/4 tbsp cranberry sauce

120 ml/4 fl oz/½ cup bottled French dressing

15 ml/1 tbsp walnut oil (optional)

Freshly ground black pepper

3 x 120 g/4½ oz small goats' cheese rounds

A little oil for greasing

1 Pile the salad leaves on six small serving plates and scatter the walnuts over.

2 Whisk the cranberry sauce with the dressing, walnut oil, if using, and a good grinding of pepper. Spoon the dressing over and around the salads.

3 Pre-heat the grill (broiler). Cut the goats' cheeses into halves and lay them on oiled foil on the grill rack. Grill (broil) for 2–3 minutes until they are beginning to melt and are lightly golden on top.

4 Quickly transfer to the salads and serve.

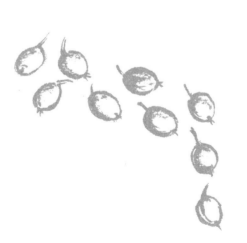

Crab and camembert parcels with avocado salsa

From the fabulous results and the taste, you wouldn't believe these parcels take only minutes to put together. The salsa adds a nice fresh touch but, if you don't want to be bothered with chopping an avocado, simply serve the parcels with a spoonful of bought guacamole instead. See photograph opposite page 24.

SERVES 6

6 sheets of filo pastry (paste)

Olive oil for brushing

2 x 200 g/7 oz/small cans of white crabmeat, drained

1 round Camembert, cut into 6 wedges

90 ml/6 tbsp crème fraîche

15 ml/1 tbsp dried Italian seasoning

Salt and freshly ground black pepper

FOR THE SALSA

1 ripe avocado

1 x 200 g/7 oz/small tub of fresh tomato salsa

6 stalks of fresh coriander (cilantro), to garnish

1 Brush the sheets of filo pastry with olive oil and fold in half widthways. Brush with a little more oil.

2 Spoon the crabmeat into the centres of each piece of folded pastry. Top with the Camembert, crème fraîche, Italian seasoning, a sprinkling of salt and a good grinding of pepper.

3 Fold the pastry over the filling to form neat parcels and transfer to an oiled baking (cookie) sheet. Brush with a little more oil.

4 To make the salsa, peel, halve, stone (pit) and finely dice the avocado. Put in a bowl. Add the tomato salsa and fold in gently. Cover and chill until ready to serve.

5 30 minutes before eating, bake the parcels in a preheated oven at 190°C/375°F/gas 5/fan oven 170°C for about 15 minutes until golden.

6 Remove from the oven and leave to cool for 10 minutes. Transfer to cool plates and spoon the salsa to one side of each. Lay a stalk of fresh coriander alongside each and serve while still warm.

Smoked salmon and cream cheese whirls

Cool green lettuce wrapped around smoked salmon filled with subtly flavoured soft white cheese. These are far more elegant than bought smoked salmon pinwheels but are created using instant ingredients. You may need to buy two round lettuces to get enough large leaves but the hearts will keep well in the salad drawer of your fridge.

SERVES 6

12 large round lettuce leaves

6 large slices of smoked salmon

200 g/7 oz/scant 1 cup medium-fat soft cheese with chives

15 ml/1 tbsp milk

1.5 ml/¼ tsp cayenne

Freshly ground black pepper

1 small packet of mixed salad leaves, including some red ones

90 ml/6 tbsp bottled French dressing

30 ml/2 tbsp sliced stoned (pitted) black olives

1 lemon cut into six wedges, to garnish

1 Trim any thick stalks from the lettuce leaves. Rinse with cold water and pat dry on kitchen paper (paper towels).

2 Cut the smoked salmon slices in halves lengthways and lay on the lettuce leaves.

3 Mix the cheese with the milk, cayenne and a good grinding of pepper. Spread over the salmon. Fold in the sides of the lettuce, then roll up tightly. Place in a covered container in the fridge until ready to serve.

4 To serve, put two rolls on each of six serving plates and cut into thick slices. Arrange attractively, slightly overlapping, then pile the leaves to one side. Spoon the dressing over the salad and scatter the olive slices over. Garnish each plate with a wedge of lemon and serve.

Prawns newburg

This is not so much a cheat as a clever way to ensure the sauce works reliably without curdling, which it can do if you use the traditional cooking method. However, it is quick and easy to make with frozen seafood and most of the ingredients will already be in your storecupboard.

SERVES 6

100 g/4 oz/½ cup wild rice

25 g/1 oz/2 tbsp butter

450 g/1 lb frozen cooked tiger prawns (shrimp), thawed

90 ml/6 tbsp medium-dry sherry

30 ml/2 tbsp bottled lemon juice

1 large egg

2.5 ml/½ tsp chilli powder

5 ml/1 tsp paprika

10 ml/2 tsp cornflour (cornstarch)

Salt and freshly ground black pepper

200 ml/7 fl oz/scant 1 cup single (light) cream

30 ml/2 tbsp chopped fresh or a little dried parsley

1 Cook the wild rice according to the packet directions. Drain.

2 Meanwhile, melt the butter in a frying pan (skillet). Add the prawns, sherry and lemon juice and simmer until the liquid has reduced by half.

3 Whisk together the remaining ingredients except the parsley and pour into the pan. Cook fairly gently, stirring, until bubbling, but do not allow to boil rapidly.

4 Spoon the wild rice into warm, shallow individual serving dishes. Spoon the prawns over, sprinkle with the chopped parsley and serve.

Warm asparagus mousse with fresh tarragon

Mousses normally involve separating eggs, delicate folding and complicated instructions. Not here – just canned asparagus puréed with eggs, cream and herbs and lightly cooked. The sauce is simply wine and cream! If you like, cook a small pack of fresh thin asparagus tips and lay a few stalks beside each mousse as a garnish.

SERVES 4

1 x 410 g/14½ oz/large can of cut asparagus spears

3 eggs

5 ml/1 tsp dried tarragon

15 ml/1 tbsp snipped fresh or 5 ml/1 tsp dried chives

300 ml/½ pt/1¼ cups single (light) cream

Salt and freshly ground black pepper

A little butter or oil for greasing

150 ml/¼ pt/⅔ cup dry white wine

5 ml/1 tsp dried minced onion

150 ml/¼ pt/⅔ cup double (heavy) cream

Snipped fresh or dried chives, to garnish

1 Drain the asparagus, reserving the liquid. Tip the asparagus into a blender or food processor with the eggs, herbs and single cream. Blend until smooth, then season to taste.

2 Grease six ramekin dishes (custard cups) and pour in the asparagus mixture. Stand the dishes in a roasting tin (pan) with enough boiling water to come half way up the sides of the dishes. Cover the tin with foil.

3 Bake in a preheated oven at 160°C/325°F/gas 3/fan oven 145°C for 1 hour or until the mousses are set.

4 Meanwhile, measure 150 ml/¼ pt/⅔ cup of the asparagus liquid into a saucepan. Add the wine and dried onion. Bring to the boil and boil for about 5 minutes or until reduced by half. Add the double cream and boil for a further 5 minutes until thickened slightly. Season to taste.

5 Carefully loosen the mousses and turn out on to warm serving plates. Spoon the sauce around. Sprinkle the mousses with a few snipped fresh or dried chives and serve.

Creamy cannellini bean and chorizo sauté

This warm, creamy yet spicy concoction tastes divine when eaten wrapped in cool lettuce leaves for the perfect combination of textures and flavours. Chorizo sausage comes ready diced or sliced so, apart from chopping an onion and a garlic clove, you have very little to do. Use the lettuce hearts in a salad.

SERVES 6–8

1 red onion, chopped

1 small garlic clove, chopped, or 2.5 ml/½ tsp garlic purée (paste)

30 ml/2 tbsp olive oil

100 g/4 oz ready diced or sliced chorizo sausage (quarter the slices if large)

2 x 425 g/15 oz/large cans of cannellini beans, drained, rinsed and drained again

60 ml/4 tbsp crème fraîche

30 ml/2 tbsp chopped fresh or frozen parsley

Salt and freshly ground black pepper

10 ml/2 tsp dried chilli flakes

1–2 round lettuces, separated into leaves (except the hearts)

1 Fry (sauté) the onion and garlic in the oil for 2 minutes. Add the chorizo and continue to fry, tossing and stirring for 2 minutes.

2 Add the beans, crème fraîche and parsley. Heat through, stirring and turning gently. Season to taste.

3 Pile into small warm bowls and sprinkle with the chilli flakes. Serve with lettuce leaves to spoon the beans into, wrap and eat.

STARTERS

Antipasto platter

This colourful mixture of sweet and savoury delicacies – all pre-packaged and ready-prepared – makes the ideal starter for any occasion, especially if you are short of time or haven't the inclination to cook. I like to drizzle it with just olive oil, but if you prefer you could use bottled French or honey and mustard dressing.

SERVES 6

2 x 85g/3½ oz packets of mixed antipasto meats (salami, Parma ham, pancetta etc.)

1 x 410 g/14 oz/large can of melon balls, drained

2 small fresh Mozarella cheeses, drained and sliced

12 black olives

12 green olives

12 cherry tomatoes, halved

45 ml/3 tbsp olive oil

Freshly ground black pepper

A few fresh basil leaves

TO SERVE
Focaccia bread and unsalted (sweet) butter

1 Arrange all the ingredients, except the oil, pepper and basil, attractively on six individual serving plates or one large platter.

2 Drizzle the oil over, add a good grinding of pepper and scatter a few basil leaves over. Serve with focaccia bread and unsalted butter.

Grilled chicken goujons with cranberry dip

*Choose best-quality chicken fillet fingers rather than ones made with minced poultry –
I'm never quite sure what they contain when the meat has been minced up! With a
little extra seasoning and served with a creamy cranberry dip, they are lifted from their
once-humble beginnings into the dinner-party class.*

SERVES 4–6

**450 g/1 lb frozen chicken fingers in
breadcrumbs or batter**

Bottled lemon juice

10 ml/2 tsp dried thyme

Salt and freshly ground black pepper

FOR THE DIP

150 ml/¼ pt/⅔ cup crème fraîche

45 ml/3 tbsp cranberry sauce

5 ml/1 tsp dried minced onion

Lemon wedges, to garnish

1 Lay the chicken fingers on foil on the grill (broiler) rack. Sprinkle each
with a few drops of lemon juice, then sprinkle with half the thyme
and a good grinding of pepper. Turn them over and repeat the
seasoning.

2 Mix together all the dip ingredients and season to taste. Tip into a
small bowl and chill until ready to serve. Preheat the grill.

3 Grill (broil) the chicken fingers, turning once or twice until crisp,
golden and cooked through.

4 Put the dish of dip in the centre of a plate and arrange the goujons
around. Garnish with wedges of lemon.

Photograph opposite:
**Crab and camembert parcels with
avocado salsa** (see page 18)
Photograph overleaf:
**Pork chops with grainy mustard jus
on rosti** (see page 26)

meat main courses

Whether you want to brighten up a pork chop or cook a gourmet-style curry, you need a great sauce. Bought ones are okay but too often they taste a bit synthetic. However, with some simple added ingredients to give them individuality and authenticity, they can be cunningly disguised. So with these and some other storecupboard additions you can create gastronomic delights that would impress even the greatest chefs. And, best of all, you most definitely won't have to spend hours slaving over a hot stove!

Pork chops with grainy mustard jus on rosti

Pork chops are so easy to cook. Here, I've flavoured them with sage and smothered them in a simple sauce made of smooth crème fraîche with wholegrain mustard and a good dash of brandy to give it a bit of a kick. Serve the pork on golden potato cakes for a complete and delicious meal. See photograph opposite page 25.

SERVES 4

4 pork chops

4 pinches of dried sage

Salt and freshly ground black pepper

A good knob of butter or margarine

15 ml/1 tbsp olive oil

4 frozen rosti

30 ml/2 tbsp brandy

200 ml/7 fl oz/scant 1 cup crème fraîche

30 ml/2 tbsp wholegrain mustard

A pinch of caster (superfine) sugar

4 sprigs of fresh parsley, to garnish

TO SERVE
Spinach or broccoli

1 Season the chops with the sage and a little salt and pepper.

2 Heat the butter or margarine and oil in a large frying pan (skillet). Add the chops and fry (sauté) quickly on both sides to brown. Turn down the heat and cook for about 15 minutes until cooked through, turning once or twice. Transfer to a plate and keep warm.

3 Meanwhile, cook the rosti under a preheated grill (broiler) until golden on both sides and cooked through. Keep warm.

4 Add the brandy to the juices in the frying pan. Stir in the crème fraîche and mustard and cook gently, stirring all the time, until bubbling and well blended. Season to taste with the sugar and salt and pepper.

5 Transfer the rosti to warm plates and top each with a chop. Pour any juices on the plate back into the sauce and stir. Spoon a little sauce over each chop and garnish each plate with a sprig of parsley. Serve with spinach or broccoli.

Pork steaks with spicy wedges and cheese and chive dip

This brilliant barbecue sauce I use to make this dish is nothing more than the bottled table variety but, once cooked, it tastes as if it took hours to prepare. Frozen potato wedges are given an exciting twist with the addition of a mixture of spices, and the dip takes just a minute or two to make.

SERVES 4

4 pork shoulder steaks

A little oil for greasing

60 ml/4 tbsp bottled barbecue table sauce

700 g/1½ lb frozen potato wedges

15 ml/1 tbsp ground cumin

15 ml/1 tbsp ground coriander (cilantro)

1.5 ml/¼ tsp chilli powder

Salt and freshly ground black pepper

200 g/7 oz/scant 1 cup medium-fat soft cheese with chives

60 ml/4 tbsp milk

TO SERVE
A mixed salad

1 Put the steaks in a lightly oiled baking tin (pan). Spread half the sauce over. Turn the steaks over and spread the other sides with the remaining sauce.

2 Cook in the centre of a preheated oven at 200°C/400°F/gas 6/fan oven 180°C for 20 minutes. Turn the steaks over.

3 Arrange the potato wedges in a separate baking tin. Mix the spices with 5 ml/1 tsp salt and a good grinding of pepper and sprinkle over. Toss with the hands to coat well.

4 Put the potatoes towards the top of the oven and continue to cook for 30 minutes, turning the wedges over once, until the potatoes are golden and the steaks are coated in a rich glaze.

5 Meanwhile, mix the cheese and chives with the milk to form a dipping sauce. Season to taste with salt and pepper. Spoon into four small pots. Transfer the steaks and potato wedges to warm plates and put a pot of dip to one side of each. Serve with a mixed salad.

Pork tenderloin wrap with cheese fondue

This is so easy – no pre-cooking and no difficult sauces. If your tenderloin is a little long for the pastry, cut off the extra piece, season it as for the rest of the meat and wrap it in oiled foil. Bake it alongside the pork roll and slice it to serve with the pastry end slices, which never seem to have much meat in them.

SERVES 4–6

450 g/1 lb pork tenderloin, trimmed of any sinews

Salt and freshly ground black pepper

5 ml/1 tsp dried thyme

1 ready-rolled sheet of frozen puff pastry (paste), thawed

12 slices of German salami

1 egg, beaten

FOR THE FONDUE
1 garlic clove, halved

100 g/4 oz/½ cup cheese spread

120 ml/4 fl oz/½ cup crème fraîche

15 ml/1 tbsp kirsch or vodka

Sprigs of fresh parsley, to garnish

TO SERVE
New potatoes and broccoli

1 Preheat the oven to 190°C/375°F/gas 5/fan oven 170°C. Season the pork all over with salt, pepper and the thyme.

2 Lay the pastry on a board. Lay half the salami slices overlapping down the centre. Top with the pork, then lay the remaining salami over to cover it completely. Brush the edges of the pastry with beaten egg.

3 Wrap the pork in the pastry and place it sealed-side down on a dampened baking (cookie) sheet. Make 11 small slashes at intervals in the pastry where it will be sliced after cooking.

4 Brush the pastry all over with beaten egg, then bake in the oven for 40 minutes until risen and golden. Leave to rest in a warm place for 5 minutes.

5 Meanwhile, rub the garlic round the inside of a small saucepan. Add the cheese, crème fraîche and kirsch or vodka. Heat through, stirring until blended, thick and smooth. Season with pepper.

6 Cut the pork roll into 12 thick slices. Lay two or three slices on each of six or four warm serving plates and spoon a little fondue over. Garnish with sprigs of parsley and serve with new potatoes and broccoli.

Succulent beef layer with crunchy water chestnuts

This is based on a recipe that traditionally takes four hours to cook initially – and that's just to tenderise the steak before putting the dish together. Here I use canned stewed steak but I promise you no one will ever guess. It's meltingly tender, rich and delicious when mixed with the rest of the ingredients.

SERVES 4

4 large potatoes, scrubbed

2 x 435 g/15 oz/large cans of stewed steak in gravy

1 x 225 g/8 oz/small can of water chestnuts, drained

100 g/4 oz button mushrooms, sliced

1 x 295 g/10½ oz/medium can of condensed cream of mushroom soup

Freshly ground black pepper

TO SERVE

Broccoli and baby carrots

1 Prick the potatoes with a fork and either bake in the microwave or boil in water for 15 minutes until almost tender. Drain, if necessary. Cut into slices.

2 Spoon the steak into a fairly shallow medium-sized ovenproof dish. Slice the water chestnuts and scatter over the surface with the mushrooms.

3 Spoon half the soup over and add a good grinding of pepper. Arrange the potato slices overlapping on the top.

4 Mix the remaining soup with 45 ml/3 tbsp water. Spread over the surface of the potatoes. Bake in a preheated oven at 200°C/400°F/gas 6/fan oven 180°C for about 45 minutes until golden on top and the potatoes are cooked through.

5 Serve hot with broccoli and baby carrots.

Braised lamb steaks with rich tomato and basil sauce

Many of the sauces in this book are made with condensed soups. Here I just use ordinary cream of tomato soup; once it's mixed with the meat juices and a little basil, the flavour is outstanding. If you like, you could try adding a swirl of soured cream or crème fraîche on each lamb steak just before serving, for added richness.

SERVES 4

4 lamb leg steaks

Salt and freshly ground black pepper

15 ml/1 tbsp olive oil

2 onions, thinly sliced

1 x 400 g/14 oz/large can of cream of tomato soup

5 ml/1 tsp dried basil

350 g/12 oz tagliatelle

A good knob of butter or margarine

30 ml/2 tbsp chopped fresh parsley, to garnish

TO SERVE
A large green salad

1 Season the steaks with a little salt and pepper. Heat the oil in a flameproof casserole dish (Dutch oven). Add the lamb steaks and brown quickly on both sides. Remove from the pan.

2 Add the onions to the pan and brown quickly for 2–3 minutes, stirring. Lay the lamb on top of the onions.

3 Spoon the soup over and sprinkle with the basil. Cover with a lid or foil and transfer to a preheated oven at 180°C/350°F/gas 4/fan oven 160°C and cook for about 1 hour or until really tender.

4 Meanwhile, cook the tagliatelle according to the packet directions. Drain thoroughly, return to the pan and toss in the butter or margarine.

5 Pile the tagliatelle on to warm serving plates. Put a lamb steak and a little of the sauce to one side. Sprinkle with parsley and serve with a large green salad.

Italian-style roast lamb with garlic flageolet

For this dish, I use the sort of Bolognese sauce you are supposed to add minced beef to for the popular spaghetti dish, but instead it's poured over the lamb for a glorious, rich, tomato-based sauce. The flavours marry perfectly. This also tastes good served with Galette Lyonnaise (see page 92).

SERVES 6

1 frozen boned and rolled shoulder of lamb, thawed

1 x 500 ml/17 fl oz jar of pasta sauce for Bolognese

30 ml/2 tbsp sliced black olives

Salt and freshly ground black pepper

2 x 350 g/12 oz/medium cans of flageolet beans

1 large garlic clove, crushed, or 5 ml/1 tsp garlic purée (paste)

15 ml/1 tbsp chopped fresh or frozen parsley

TO SERVE

Ciabatta bread and a green salad

1 Preheat the oven to 160°C/325°F/gas 3/fan oven 145°C. Put the lamb in a large shallow casserole dish (Dutch oven), pour the sauce over and add the olives. Season with salt and pepper.

2 Cover and cook in the oven for 3 hours.

3 Meanwhile mix the beans with the garlic and a little salt and pepper in a smaller ovenproof dish. Cover and place in the oven for the last 45 minutes to heat through. Drain and stir in the parsley.

4 Lift the lamb out of the sauce and cut into thick slices. Arrange on warm plates. Spoon off any excess fat from the sauce, stir and spoon the sauce over the lamb. Pile the beans to one side. Serve with ciabatta bread and a green salad.

Cassoulet

The traditional version of this rustic dish usually takes hours to prepare and cook –
but we can change that with my quick version. You'll still be able to serve a rich
mixture of meats and beans flavoured with vegetables and herbs, which makes a
wonderfully easy, hearty meal.

MEAT MAIN COURSES

SERVES 4

15 ml/1 tbsp olive oil

1 onion, chopped

1 carrot, chopped

2 celery sticks, chopped

2 garlic cloves, crushed, or
7.5 ml/1½ tsp garlic purée (paste)

4 slices of belly pork

225 g/8 oz pork chipolata sausages

4 chicken legs

2 x 425 g/15 oz/large cans of haricot
(navy) beans, drained

450 ml/¾ pt/2 cups chicken stock,
made with 1 stock cube

15 ml/1 tbsp golden (light corn) syrup

5 ml/1 tsp Dijon mustard

Salt and freshly ground black pepper

1 bouquet garni sachet

2 Weetabix

50 g/2 oz/½ cup grated Cheddar cheese

A little chopped fresh or dried parsley,
to garnish

TO SERVE
French bread and a green salad

1 Heat the oil in a flameproof casserole dish (Dutch oven). Add the onion, carrot, celery and garlic and fry (sauté) for 2 minutes, stirring.

2 Cut the pork into chunks, discarding the rind and bones, and halve the sausages. Add to the casserole with the chicken and cook, stirring and turning for a few minutes to brown.

3 Add the beans, stock, syrup, mustard, a little salt and pepper and the bouquet garni. Bring to the boil, stir, then put on the lid.

4 Transfer to a preheated oven at 180°C/350°F/gas 4/fan oven 160°C for 1 hour.

5 Crush the Weetabix and mix with the cheese.

6 Taste the cassoulet and re-season, if necessary. Discard the bouquet garni. Turn up the oven to 200°C/400°F/gas 6/fan oven 180°C.

7 Sprinkle the cheese mixture over the surface and return to the oven for 15 minutes until golden.

8 Sprinkle with the parsley and serve hot with French bread and a green salad.

Swiss steak with baby jackets

This casserole tastes so rich and delicious, you'd think it took hours to prepare. The trick is that there's no fiddly preparation or pre-cooking of any of the ingredients. You simply chuck in all the meat and vegetables, stir them together, add some seasoning and let it cook – it couldn't be easier!

SERVES 4

700 g/1½ lb diced stewing steak, trimmed of excess fat and any gristle

1 bunch of spring onions (scallions), trimmed and chopped

1 garlic clove, crushed, or 5 ml/1 tsp garlic purée (paste)

1 x 400 g/14 oz/large can of chopped tomatoes

100 g/4 oz baby button mushrooms or 1 x 300 g/11 oz/medium can, drained

45 ml/3 tbsp tomato purée (paste)

5 ml/1 tsp caster (superfine) sugar

2.5 ml/½ tsp dried mixed herbs

5 ml/1 tsp celery salt

Freshly ground black pepper

12 small potatoes, scrubbed

A little sunflower oil

60 ml/4 tbsp soured (dairy sour) cream

A little dried parsley, to garnish

TO SERVE
Broccoli and mangetout (snow peas)

1 Mix together the meat, spring onions, garlic, tomatoes, mushrooms, tomato purée, sugar, herbs, the celery salt and a good grinding of pepper in a casserole dish (Dutch oven). Place in a preheated oven at 160°C/325°F/gas 3/fan oven 140°C and cook for 2½ hours, stirring once or twice.

2 Meanwhile, rub the potatoes with a little oil and salt and place on a baking (cookie) sheet. Bake towards the top of the oven for the last hour of cooking.

3 Spoon the casserole on to warm plates. Add a swirl of soured cream to each and dust the edges of the plates with a little dried parsley. Serve with the potatoes, broccoli and mangetout.

Lamb tagine with apricots and couscous

Using frozen diced lamb saves time and effort when you are cooking, and canned apricots give the delicious sweet flavour so popular in Moroccan cooking. There is no pre-cooking necessary either; simply mix and cook, but your guests will be convinced you've been taking lessons in North African cooking!

SERVES 4

700 g/1½ lb frozen diced stewing lamb, thawed

5 ml/1 tsp ground cinnamon

5 ml/1 tsp ground ginger

5 ml/1 tsp ground cumin

2.5 ml/½ tsp salt

1 garlic clove, crushed, or 5 ml/1 tsp garlic purée (paste)

1 onion, chopped

Freshly ground black pepper

1 x 410 g/14 oz/large can of apricot halves

450 ml/¾ pt/2 cups lamb or vegetable stock, made with 1 stock cube

30 ml/2 tbsp tomato purée (paste)

225 g/8 oz/1⅓ cups couscous

30 ml/2 tbsp chopped fresh coriander (cilantro), to garnish

1 Put the meat with all the spices, the salt, garlic, onion and a good grinding of pepper in a flameproof casserole dish (Dutch oven). Toss with your hands to coat completely.

2 Stir in the apricots and their juice, the stock and tomato purée. Bring to the boil, cover, reduce the heat and simmer gently for 1½–2 hours until the meat is really tender, stirring once or twice. Taste and re-season if necessary.

3 Meanwhile, cook the couscous according to the packet directions. Fluff up with a fork.

4 Spoon the couscous on to warm plates and top with the tagine. Sprinkle with the coriander and serve.

Rustic rigatoni on crunchy courgette ribbons

Some people might balk at using canned minced beef, but for this dish it really does give excellent results as long as you make sure you use good-quality minced steak. It makes it taste like an authentic Italian speciality and I guarantee you'll love the results. It really couldn't be simpler or more delicious.

SERVES 4

225 g/8 oz rigatoni

1 x 425 g/15 oz/large can of minced steak with onions

5 ml/1 tsp dried mixed herbs

50 g/2 oz/¹⁄₂ cup grated Cheddar cheese

50 g/2 oz/¹⁄₂ cup grated Mozzarella cheese

4 large courgettes (zucchini)

15 ml/1 tbsp olive oil

15 g/¹⁄₂ oz/1 tbsp butter or margarine

60 ml/4 tbsp fresh breadcrumbs

1 Cook the pasta according to the packet directions. Drain and return to the pan.

2 Stir in the meat and herbs and heat through, stirring.

3 Preheat the grill (broiler). Spoon the mixture into a flameproof serving dish and top with the cheeses. Cook under the grill until golden and bubbling.

4 Meanwhile, pare the courgettes into long ribbons with a potato peeler. Cook in boiling lightly salted water for 2 minutes, then drain. (Alternatively place them in a steamer over the pan of pasta while it's cooking for 2–3 minutes.)

5 Heat the oil and butter or maragarine in a frying pan (skillet). Add the breadcrumbs and cook, stirring, until crisp and golden. Add the courgettes and toss to coat completely.

6 Pile the courgette ribbons on to warm plates. Top each with a quarter of the pasta bake and serve.

Beef wellington without the fuss

This is a dinner-party classic that many people buy from a supermarket rather than make themselves because they think it's too complicated. I guarantee my simple version will impress even the most discerning of guests. When wrapping the meat in pastry, imagine you are wrapping up a present, and tuck any joins underneath.

SERVES 6

25 g/1 oz/2 tbsp butter

6 small fillet steaks, about 100 g/4 oz each

350 g/12 oz frozen puff pastry (paste), thawed

225 g/8 oz smooth liver pâté

6 good pinches of dried thyme

Salt and freshly ground black pepper

1 egg, beaten

2 x 170 g/6 oz/small cans of creamed mushrooms

45 ml/3 tbsp milk

15 ml/1 tbsp brandy

Sprigs of fresh parsley, to garnish

TO SERVE
A selection of baby vegetables

1 Melt the butter in a frying pan (skillet). Add the steaks and brown quickly on both sides. Remove from the heat.

2 Cut the pastry into six equal portions and roll out each to an 18 cm/7 in square.

3 Spread the pâté over the centre of each square, top with the steaks, then sprinkle with the thyme and a little salt and pepper.

4 Brush the edges of the pastry with water and wrap over the meat to form sealed parcels.

5 Place sealed-sides down on a dampened baking (cookie) sheet and brush with beaten egg to glaze. Make any pastry trimmings into leaves, arrange on top and brush with more egg.

6 Bake in a preheated oven at 220°C/425°F/gas 7/fan oven 200°C for 20 minutes until puffy and golden brown.

7 Meanwhile, put the mushrooms in a saucepan with the milk and brandy. Heat through, stirring. Transfer the pies to warm plates, spoon the sauce to one side and garnish each plate with sprigs of parsley. Serve with baby vegetables.

Fast thai-style red beef and potato curry

Using tender good-quality steak may be more expensive than some other cuts, but it means you can cook a Thai curry with a really authentic flavour in next to no time. You can buy a cook-in red curry sauce, but this is cheaper and just as easy. Add a handful of raw cashew nuts with the tomatoes if you like them.

SERVES 4

450 g/1 lb lean sirloin or rump steak

15 ml/1 tbsp sesame or sunflower oil

1 onion, chopped

45 ml/3 tbsp Thai red curry paste

1 x 400 ml/14 fl oz/large can of coconut milk

2 large potatoes, peeled and each cut into 6 chunks

3 tomatoes, quartered

A few torn coriander (cilantro) leaves, to garnish

TO SERVE

Thai jasmine rice or Chinese egg noodles

1 Cut the meat into small cubes, discarding any fat or gristle.

2 Heat the oil in a large frying pan (skillet). Add the onion and meat and stir-fry for 2 minutes, turning the cubes of steak over until browned on all sides.

3 Add the curry paste and fry 30 seconds, then stir in the coconut milk and potatoes. Bring to the boil, stirring, then turn down the heat, cover and simmer very gently for 35 minutes.

4 Add the tomatoes and simmer uncovered for a further 5 minutes until the potatoes and beef are tender and the tomatoes are cooked but still have some shape. The sauce should still be fairly thin.

5 Serve garnished with a few torn coriander leaves on a bed of Thai jasmine rice or Chinese egg noodles.

Sautéed steak with creamy pepper sauce

Soft cheese with peppercorns makes the perfect sauce for steak, which is quick and easy to cook to perfection. Simply thin the soft cheese with a little milk and stir it into the cooking juices. It tastes just like a restaurant speciality but it is so easy you simply can't get it wrong!

SERVES 4

4 thin frying (sautéing) steaks

Salt and freshly ground black pepper

A little bottled lemon juice

15 ml/1 tbsp olive oil

15 g/½ oz/1 tbsp butter

80 g/3¼ oz/1 small pack of medium-fat soft cheese with black pepper

45 ml/3 tbsp milk

A little chopped fresh or dried parsley, to garnish

TO SERVE

Golden Glazed Potatoes (see page 89) and mangetout (snow peas)

1 Put the steaks one at a time in a plastic bag and beat with a rolling pin or meat mallet to flatten and tenderise. Season with salt and pepper and add a sprinkling of lemon juice.

2 Heat the oil and butter in a large frying pan (skillet). Add the steaks and fry (sauté) for 1–2 minutes until browned (you may need to cook them two at a time). Turn them over and cook the other sides. Transfer to a plate and keep warm.

3 Add the cheese to the pan juices with the milk and cook gently, stirring all the time, until blended and a rich, smooth sauce is formed. Add a dash more milk if necessary.

4 Transfer the steaks to warm serving plates. Pour any steak juices from the plate back into the sauce and stir in. Spoon over the steaks and sprinkle with chopped parsley. Serve with Golden Glazed Potatoes and mangetout.

Nutty mint-glazed lamb with cheesy hash potatoes

The nutty glaze in this recipe is no more than bottled mint jelly, ready-chopped nuts and a hint of garlic. The steaks are served on bought hash browns baked with a cheese topping – ridiculously easy, remarkably good! If you don't like nuts, simply glaze with the mint jelly and garlic.

SERVES 4

4 lamb shoulder or chump steaks

60 ml/4 tbsp mint jelly

60 ml/4 tbsp chopped mixed nuts

1 small garlic clove, crushed, or 2.5 ml/½ tsp garlic purée (paste)

15 g/½ oz/1 tbsp butter for greasing

1 x 700 g/1½ lb bag frozen hash browns

100 g/4 oz/1 cup grated Cheddar cheese

300 ml/½ pt/1¼ cups lamb or beef stock, made with 1 stock cube

Salt and freshly ground black pepper

Dried parsley, to garnish

TO SERVE
Peas and baby carrots

1 Preheat the oven to 200°C/400°F/gas 6/fan oven 180°C. Trim any excess fat from the steaks. Melt the jelly in a small saucepan and stir in the nuts and garlic. Brush all over the steaks on both sides.

2 Grease a baking tin (pan) with the butter. Lay the steaks in it.

3 Lay the hash browns in a shallow rectangular ovenproof serving dish, arranging them so they fit together neatly side by side. Place the hash browns on the top shelf of the oven and the lamb on the shelf just above the centre. Bake for 15 minutes.

4 Scatter the cheese evenly all over the top of the hash browns, return to the oven and bake for a further 15 minutes until golden and bubbling and the meat is tender and richly glazed. Leave the cheese hash in the oven while you prepare the jus. Carefully lift the meat out of the dish and keep warm.

5 Pour the stock into the pan and boil rapidly, scraping up any sediment, until slightly thickened and reduced. Season to taste.

6 Cut the hash brown 'cake' into four portions and transfer a portion to each of four warm plates. Rest the lamb steaks against the 'cakes' and spoon the jus over. Dust the edge of the plate with dried parsley and serve with peas and baby carrots.

One-step choucroute garni

You can buy this delicious dish in many French street markets. Making it normally takes ages and involves long, very slow cooking. Here the ingredients are simply mixed together and baked for just 1 hour (but it can sit in the oven for a lot longer if necessary). It is almost indistinguishable from the real thing but is a total cheat.

SERVES 4

700 g/1½ lb jar sauerkraut, drained

1 smoked pork ring, cut into chunks

450 g/1 lb piece of cooked smoked pork loin, cut into large chunks

4 fatty thick unsmoked streaky bacon rashers (slices), cut into chunks

150 ml/¼ pt/⅔ cup dry white wine

150 ml/¼ pt/⅔ cup chicken stock, made with ½ stock cube

2 cloves

1 bay leaf

Salt and freshly ground black pepper

A little chopped fresh or dried parsley, to garnish

TO SERVE
Plain boiled potatoes and mustard

1 Preheat the oven to 180°C/350°F/gas 4/fan oven 160°C. Put all the ingredients except the salt and pepper and parsley in a casserole dish (Dutch oven). Season lightly with salt and add lots of pepper.

2 Cover and bake in the oven for 1 hour. Remove the cloves and bay leaf, taste and re-season if necessary. Sprinkle with parsley and serve with plain boiled potatoes and mustard.

poultry main courses

Chicken, duck and turkey are all firm favourites for a variety of meals but they often require complicated sauces to make them really sumptuous. Here I've used a mixture of bought ones (tarted up so no one would know), storecupboard classics such as canned tomatoes, soups and savoury rices, and simple fresh ingredients that are readily available to create some fabulous culinary delights.

Chicken in pancetta with tomato and cucumber sauce

For this Italian-inspired dish, chicken breasts are wrapped in pre-packed pancetta slices and fried until golden, then served with a sauce that is simply made from a jar of tomato and Mascarpone sauce for pasta, diced cucumber and all the delicious cooking juices.

SERVES 4

8 thin slices of pancetta

4 skinless chicken breasts

30 ml/2 tbsp olive oil

¼ cucumber

1 x 190 g/6¾ oz jar of vine-ripened tomato and Mascarpone stir-through

60 ml/4 tbsp milk

Freshly ground black pepper

8 fresh basil leaves, chopped (optional)

TO SERVE
Buttered noodles and a green salad

1 Wrap two pieces of pancetta round each chicken breast to cover them as much as possible.

2 Heat the oil in a frying pan (skillet). Add the chicken and brown quickly all over. Turn down the heat, cover the pan with a lid or foil and cook very gently for 30 minutes, turning the chicken over once during cooking.

3 Carefully lift the chicken out of the pan and keep warm.

4 Cut off six thin slices of cucumber and reserve for garnishing. Finely dice the remainder and add to the pan. Cook, tossing, for 1 minute. Add the tomato and Mascarpone stir-through and thin with the milk. Season to taste with pepper and add the basil, if using. Cook, stirring, for 2 minutes until blended and bubbling.

5 Transfer the chicken to warm plates and spoon a little of the sauce over. Garnish each plate with a twist of cucumber and serve with buttered noodles and a green salad.

Warm chargrilled chicken caesar salad

Crisp cos lettuce tossed in a creamy garlic dressing with Parmesan shavings and crunchy croûtons – made by opening a few packets! – is here topped with succulent chargrilled chicken breasts courtesy of the freezer cabinet. The result is magnificent and as good as you'll get in any brasserie! See photograph opposite page 48.

SERVES 4

4 frozen chargrilled chicken breasts

2 x 250 g/9 oz packets of fresh Caesar salad

50 g/2 oz/¹⁄₂ cup black stoned (pitted) olives, chopped

50 g/2 oz/¹⁄₂ cup green stoned olives, chopped

4 cherry tomatoes, sliced

1 Cook the chicken according to the packet directions.

2 Empty the cos lettuce from the Caesar salad packs into a large bowl. Add the dressing from the sachets and the croûtons and toss gently.

3 Pile the salad on to four large serving plates. Scatter the chopped olives round the edge of the plates.

4 Cut each chicken breast into six diagonal slices but leave in their original shape and lay on top of the salads.

5 Lay the tomato slices in a cluster to one side of each plate. Scatter the Parmesan shavings from the salad packs over. Serve while the chicken is still warm.

Marinated pesto chicken on tomato bulgar

This is a succulent, fragrant and very tasty dish with a distinctly Mediterranean flavour. All you need is a few bottled, canned and packet ingredients and four chicken portions. Don't be fooled by how easy it is to put together – it will taste good enough to serve for a family meal or even a dinner party.

SERVES 4

15 ml/1 tbsp cornflour (cornstarch)

15 ml/1 tbsp water

45 ml/3 tbsp bottled pesto

30 ml/2 tbsp white wine or apple juice

15 ml/1 tbsp bottled lemon juice

Salt and freshly ground black pepper

4 chicken portions

FOR THE BULGAR

1 x 400 g/14 oz/large can of chopped tomatoes

100 g/4 oz/²⁄₃ cup bulgar (cracked wheat)

Sprigs of fresh basil, to garnish (optional)

1 Mix the cornflour with the water in a shallow dish, then stir in the pesto, wine or apple juice, the lemon juice and a little salt and pepper. Add the chicken, turn to coat completely and leave to marinate for at least 1 hour, preferably overnight.

2 Lift the chicken out of the marinade and place, skin-sides down, on foil on a grill (broiler) rack. Grill (broil) for 20 minutes, brushing once or twice with the marinade. Turn the chicken over and grill for a further 20 minutes, brushing frequently with any remaining marinade, until golden and cooked through.

3 Meanwhile, empty the tomatoes into a saucepan and add half a canful of water. Bring to the boil and stir in the bulgar. Simmer for 20 minutes, stirring occasionally, until the bulgar is swollen and has absorbed the liquid. Season to taste.

4 Spoon the tomato bulgar on to warm plates and add the chicken and any juices. Garnish with sprigs of basil, if liked, and serve.

Chicken pilaf

For a fast and delicious supper dish with the minimum of fuss, all you need is a packet of flavoured rice, some chicken and the judicious use of herbs and spices. With these few ingredients – and a little of my know-how – you can make a pilaf as good as any you'd spend hours over.

SERVES 4

350 g/12 oz chicken stir-fry meat

1 small garlic clove, crushed, or 2.5 ml/½ tsp garlic purée (paste)

25 g/1 oz/2 tbsp butter or margarine

5 ml/1 tsp ground cumin

1 packet of dried savoury rice with vegetables

30 ml/2 tbsp chopped fresh parsley or coriander (cilantro)

1 Stir-fry the chicken and garlic in the butter or margarine for 3 minutes. Stir in the cumin.

2 Add the rice to the chicken and toss until well mixed. Add boiling water, according to the packet directions. Bring to the boil, reduce the heat, part-cover and simmer for 20 minutes until the chicken is cooked and the rice is tender and has absorbed the liquid.

3 Pile on to warm plates and sprinkle with the parsley or coriander.

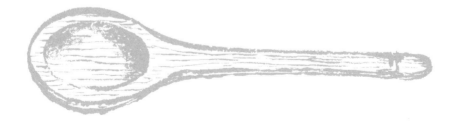

Chicken and spiced almond salad

This is an elegant dish of chicken, bathed in a smooth tomato mayonnaise, topped with warm buttery spiced almonds on crisp, colourful salad. It is ideal if you need to grab something for supper on the way home. If you don't want to cut up a chicken, use cooked portions instead, though they tend not to be so moist and flavoursome.

SERVES 4

1 small ready-cooked chicken

50 g/2 oz/½ cup blanched whole almonds

15 g/½ oz/1 tbsp butter

1.5 ml/¼ tsp chilli powder

1.5 ml/¼ tsp ground cumin

1.5 ml/¼ tsp ground cinnamon

¼ cucumber, cut into small chunks

12 cherry tomatoes, halved

1 bunch of spring onions (scallions), chopped

1 round lettuce, torn into bite-sized pieces

FOR THE DRESSING
150 ml/¼ pt/⅔ cup mayonnaise

30 ml/2 tbsp milk

15 ml/1 tbsp tomato ketchup (catsup)

A few drops of Worcestershire sauce (optional)

1 Cut the chicken into quarters.

2 Fry (sauté) the almonds in the butter for 2 minutes, stirring and tossing until golden brown. Remove from the heat and sprinkle with the spices. Toss well and drain on kitchen paper (paper towels).

3 Arrange the salad stuffs on four serving plates. Mix the dressing ingredients together.

4 Put the chicken on the salads, spoon the dressing over and scatter the warm almonds on top.

English-style roast stuffed chicken breasts

Chicken breasts, filled with stuffing mix and wrapped in bacon, give you all the traditional flavours in one go and produce glorious, moist results. This is a really attractive way to serve a roast meal with hardly any effort; you don't even have to peel the potatoes or carve the meat!

SERVES 6

1x 85 g/3½ oz packet of sage and onion stuffing mix

6 large skinless chicken breasts

6 unsmoked streaky bacon rashers (slices), rinded

60 ml/4 tbsp sunflower oil

12 smallish potatoes, scrubbed

Salt and freshly ground black pepper

30 ml/2 tbsp plain (all-purpose) flour

600 ml/1 pt/2½ cups chicken stock, made with 1 stock cube

TO SERVE
Peas and carrots

1 Make up the stuffing mix according to the packet directions. Preheat the oven to 190°C/375°F/gas 5/fan oven 170°C.

2 Make a slit in the side of each chicken breast and pack the stuffing inside. Stretch the rashers with the back of a knife and wrap one round each chicken breast.

3 Lay the chicken in a small roasting tin (pan). Drizzle with half the oil.

4 Halve the potatoes and put in a smaller roasting tin. Drizzle with the remaining oil, toss with your hands so each piece of potato is coated and sprinkle with salt. Put the potatoes on the top shelf of the oven and the chicken on the shelf just above the centre. Roast in the oven for 50–60 minutes until golden and cooked through.

5 Carefully lift the chicken out of the tin and keep warm. Sprinkle the flour into the tin and stir until blended with the cooking juices. Blend in the chicken stock. Bring to the boil and cook for 2 minutes, stirring all the time, until thickened. Taste and re-season if necessary.

6 Transfer the chicken to warm serving plates with the potatoes. Spoon a little gravy over and serve with peas and carrots.

Chicken chow mein in an instant

If you don't have leftover cooked chicken, use any bought cooked chicken meat for this simplest of dishes with a truly authentic flavour – at a fraction of the cost of a take-away! You can use frozen or fresh pre-prepared stir-fry vegetables instead of the can, and a sachet of chow mein stir-fry sauce instead of storecupboard ingredients.

SERVES 4

2 slabs of Chinese egg noodles

225 g/8 oz cooked chicken, cut into strips

1 small garlic clove, crushed, or 2.5 ml/½ tsp garlic purée (paste)

1 x 425 g/15 oz/large can of stir-fry vegetables, drained

50 g/2 oz/½ cup frozen peas

30 ml/2 tbsp soy sauce

30 ml/2 tbsp medium-dry sherry

5 ml/1 tsp ground ginger

15 ml/1 tbsp clear honey

TO SERVE
Prawn crackers

1 Cook the noodles according to the packet directions. Drain.

2 Meanwhile, put the remaining ingredients in a saucepan or wok and heat through, stirring and tossing.

3 Add the noodles and toss well. Serve in bowls with prawn crackers.

Photograph opposite:
Warm chargrilled chicken caesar salad (see page 43)

Chicken maryland with spiced fried bananas

If you cook this dish from scratch it's a lot of soaking, coating, tossing and messing around. With my cheats' version, you just use good-quality crumb-coated portions, which taste good and with these tasty accompaniments make a really authentic-tasting American-style chicken dish.

SERVES 4

4 crumb-coated chicken portions

8 streaky bacon rashers (slices), rinded

15 g/¹⁄₂ oz/1 tbsp butter

15 ml/1 tbsp sunflower oil

4 small bananas, halved lengthways

1.5 ml/¹⁄₄ tsp mixed (apple pie) spice

1.5 ml/¹⁄₄ tsp chilli powder

Watercress, to garnish

TO SERVE
Corn and Chive Fritters (see page 87), potato wedges and peas

1 Lay the chicken in a baking tin (pan). Roll up the rashers of bacon and put in a separate small tin.

2 Cook the chicken in the oven according to the manufacturers instructions. Place the bacon in the oven after 15 minutes.

3 Heat the butter and oil in a frying pan (skillet). Add the bananas and sprinkle with the spices. Fry (sauté) for 1–2 minutes on each side until golden but still holding their shape.

4 Transfer the chicken, bacon and bananas to warm serving plates. Garnish with watercress and serve with Corn and Chive Fritters, potato wedges and peas.

Photograph opposite:
Cod and bacon kebabs with rosemary dressing (see page 58)

Chicken teriyaki with sesame rice noodles and crispy ginger

The marinade is simply the bottled sauce with a dash of sherry – it's the clever flavouring of the noodles and the classy topping that makes this dish a gourmet treat. It is lovely served with a beansprout and shredded red and green pepper salad, dressed with soy sauce, lemon juice and sunflower oil.

SERVES 4

4 chicken breasts with skin

120 ml/4 fl oz/½ cup bought teriyaki sauce

30 ml/2 tbsp medium-dry sherry

75 ml/5 tbsp sunflower oil, plus extra for frying

225 g/8 oz rice noodles

10 ml/2 tsp sesame oil

1 bunch of spring onions (scallions), trimmed and finely chopped

30 ml/2 tbsp sesame seeds

1 x 50 g/2 oz packet of pickled sliced ginger

1 Lay the chicken breasts in a shallow dish and make several slashes through the skin in the flesh. Add the teriyaki sauce and sherry, turn to coat completely and leave to marinate for 1 hour.

2 Heat 30 ml/2 tbsp of the sunflower oil in a shallow pan or wok. Remove the chicken breasts from the marinade, lay skin-sides down in the pan and cook for 7–8 minutes until richly golden underneath. Turn over and cook for a further 7–8 minutes until cooked through.

3 Drain off any fat in the pan, then pour in the teriyaki marinade. Allow to bubble for several minutes, turning the chicken once until coated in the sauce.

4 Meanwhile, cook the noodles according to the packet directions. Drain thoroughly and place in a bowl.

5 Heat the remaining sunflower oil with the sesame oil in a frying pan (skillet). Add the spring onions and sesame seeds and cook, stirring, until the seeds are golden. Add to the noodles and toss well. Keep warm.

6 Drain the ginger and pat dry on kitchen paper (paper towels). Wipe out the frying pan and add about 1 cm/½ in sunflower oil. Heat the oil until a cube of day-old bread browns in 30 seconds. Add the ginger and fry (sauté) for 1–2 minutes until crisp and golden. Drain on kitchen paper.

7 Pile the noodles on to warm plates and top each pile with a chicken breast and any sauce. Top with the crispy ginger and serve.

Chicken in red wine

Succulent chicken cooked in a rich red wine sauce, laced with brandy and enhanced with mushrooms and smoky bacon. Sounds tricky? It isn't; you just brown the chicken, add everything else and pop it in the oven for an hour. The potatoes take only a few minutes to prepare just before serving. Delicious and very impressive.

SERVES 6

15 g/½ oz/1 tbsp butter or margarine

6 chicken breasts or portions with skin

150 g/5 oz baby button mushrooms or 1 x 300 g/11 oz/medium can, drained

1 x 500 g/17 oz/large can of red wine cook-in sauce

30 ml/2 tbsp brandy

7.5 ml/1½ tsp caster (superfine) sugar

2.5 ml/½ tsp dried mixed herbs

Salt and freshly ground black pepper

1 x 70 g/2¾ oz/small pack of smoked lardons (diced bacon)

A little chopped fresh or dried parsley, to garnish

TO SERVE
Creamed Potatoes (see page 89) and a green salad

1 Preheat the oven to 180°C/350°F/gas 4/fan oven 160°C. Melt the butter or margarine in a flameproof casserole dish (Dutch oven). Add the chicken, skin-sides down, and fry (sauté) for 2–3 minutes until the skin is turning golden. Turn the chicken over.

2 Add the mushrooms, then the remaining ingredients except the lardons, seasoning with just a pinch of salt and a good grinding of pepper. Stir round the chicken to mix them together a bit. Sprinkle the lardons over the surface.

3 Cover and cook in the oven for 1 hour. Stir again.

4 Sprinkle the chicken with parsley and serve with Creamed Potatoes and a green salad.

Duck breasts with golden polenta and tomato and plum salsa

The sweet, fruity salsa offsets the richness of the duck and the golden polenta adds texture and a slight blandness that also complements the meat perfectly. What's more, you don't even have to make the polenta; it's the ready-cooked variety you buy in a slab – so no effort at all!

SERVES 4

FOR THE SALSA

1 x 225 g/8 oz/small can of chopped tomatoes

1 small garlic clove, crushed, or 2.5 ml/½ tsp garlic purée (paste)

15 ml/1 tbsp tomato purée

45 ml/3 tbsp plum jam (conserve)

15 ml/1 tbsp soy sauce

FOR THE POLENTA

1 block of ready-made polenta

5 ml/1 tsp dried basil

45 ml/3 tbsp olive oil

FOR THE DUCK

4 duck breasts with skin

Salt and freshly ground black pepper

Watercress, to garnish

1 To make the salsa, put all the ingredients in a small saucepan and bring to the boil, stirring. Boil for 2 minutes, then remove from the heat.

2 To make the polenta, cut the block into 12 slices. Sprinkle with the basil. Fry (sauté) in the olive oil for about 2 minutes on each side until golden. Drain on kitchen paper (paper towels) and keep warm.

3 Season the duck with salt and pepper and score the skin with a sharp knife in a criss-cross pattern. Heat a non-stick frying pan (skillet) and fry the duck breasts, skin-sides, down for 4 minutes until golden and the fat has run. Turn over and cook for a further 3 minutes until cooked but still slightly pink in the centre.

4 Arrange the polenta slices overlapping in a pile on four warm serving plates. Put the duck breasts alongside.

5 Put a spoonful of the salsa on each plate and garnish with a little watercress.

Duck breasts with calvados and apple and sage rice

I find microwave rice works very well and is quick and easy to cook. If you don't have a microwave oven, you can heat the rice in a steamer or metal colander over a pan of simmering water for several minutes until piping hot. If you don't have Calvados, you can use brandy instead.

SERVES 4

4 duck breasts with skin

Salt and freshly ground black pepper

250 ml/8 fl oz/1 cup chicken stock, made with ½ stock cube

45 ml/3 tbsp Calvados

15 ml/1 tbsp tomato purée (paste)

5 ml/1 tsp caster (superfine) sugar

A good knob of butter

1 x 250 g/9 oz packet of microwave long-grain rice

30 ml/2 tbsp bottled apple sauce

5 ml/1 tsp dried sage

5 ml/1 tsp dried chives

TO SERVE
Peas

1 Season the duck with salt and pepper and score the skin with a sharp knife in a criss-cross pattern. Heat a non-stick frying pan (skillet), add the duck breasts, skin-sides down, and fry (sauté) gently until the fat starts to run. Turn up the heat and fry for 4 minutes until the skin is richly browned. Turn over, turn down the heat to moderate and fry for a further 3 minutes. Remove from the pan and keep warm. Pour off all but 15 ml/1 tbsp of the fat.

2 Stir the stock into the pan and bring to the boil, stirring and scraping up any sediment. Stir in the Calvados, tomato purée and sugar, bring to the boil and boil rapidly for 2–3 minutes until slightly reduced. Whisk in the butter to thicken slightly. Season to taste with salt, if necessary, and a good grinding of pepper.

3 Meanwhile, microwave the rice according to the manufacturer's instructions. Fork it well to loosen the grains. Add the apple sauce, sage, chives and seasoning to taste. Stir well with a fork, then heat through for a further 1 minute in the microwave.

4 Pile the rice on to warm plates. Cut the duck into six diagonal slices and lay to one side. Spoon the sauce over and serve with peas.

Crunchy turkey escalopes with carrot and potato mash

*A simple stuffing mix makes a delicious crunchy coating for turkey, pork or chicken –
and not even a breadcrumb has to be made! It doesn't have to be parsley and
thyme, either; try apricot and nut or sage and onion. Serve it with this delicious purée
– no peeling or boiling needed – to add the perfect moist accompaniment.*

SERVES 4

4 turkey breast steaks

5 ml/1 tsp dried chilli flakes

**1 x 85 g/3½ oz packet of parsley, thyme
and lemon stuffing mix**

1 egg, beaten

Oil for shallow-frying

FOR THE MASH

**4-portion quantity of instant
mashed potato flakes**

45 ml/3 tbsp dried milk powder

A good knob of butter

**1 x 295 g/10½ oz/medium can of
carrots, drained**

5 ml/1 tsp dried chives

**Lemon wedges and sprigs of parsley,
to garnish**

TO SERVE
French (green) beans

1 Put the turkey steaks one at a time in a plastic bag and beat with a rolling pin or meat mallet to flatten. Stir the chilli flakes into the stuffing mix.

2 Dip the steaks in the beaten egg, then the stuffing mix to coat completely.

3 Heat enough oil to cover the base of a large frying pan (skillet). Add the turkey escalopes and fry (sauté) for 3 minutes on each side until golden brown and cooked through. Drain on kitchen paper (paper towels).

4 Empty the potato flakes into a saucepan, add the milk powder and make up with boiling water according to the packet directions. Add the butter, carrots and chives. Mash with a potato masher until well blended, then heat through, stirring.

5 Spoon the mash on to warm plates and lay a turkey escalope alongside. Garnish the plates with wedges of lemon and sprigs of parsley and serve with French beans.

Mock peking duck

This is a tasty alternative to the original. It's a more filling version for a whole meal and takes far less work and time to prepare. Use bought plum sauce if you prefer, but this uses ingredients you may well have in your storecupboard and you will find that – like every recipe in this book – it is quick and easy to make.

SERVES 4

12 spring onions (scallions)

½ cucumber

450 g/1 lb turkey stir-fry pieces

FOR THE MARINADE
30 ml/2 tbsp soy sauce

2.5 ml/½ tsp ground ginger

1 small garlic clove, crushed, or
2.5 ml/½ tsp garlic purée (paste)

15 ml/1 tbsp red wine vinegar

FOR THE SAUCE
60 ml/4 tbsp plum jam (conserve)

30 ml/2 tbsp soy sauce

5 ml/1 tsp ground ginger

5 ml/1 tsp lemon juice

TO FINISH
15 ml/1 tbsp sunflower oil

12 flour tortillas

TO SERVE
A mixed salad

1 Trim the roots and tops off the spring onions. Make several cuts through the white bulb to a depth of about 2.5 cm/1 in. Place in a bowl of cold water to open out.

2 Cut the cucumber into matchsticks. Place in a serving bowl and chill.

3 Put the turkey in a shallow dish. Mix together the marinade ingredients and pour over the turkey. Toss well and leave to marinate for 1 hour.

4 Mix together the sauce ingredients in a small bowl.

5 Heat the oil in a large frying pan (skillet) or wok. Add the turkey and stir-fry for about 5 minutes until cooked through. Turn into a serving dish.

6 Meanwhile, warm the tortillas according to the packet directions. Drain the spring onions.

7 To serve, use a spring onion 'brush' to spread a little of the plum sauce on a tortilla. Lay the onion on top. Top with some turkey and a little cucumber. Roll up and enjoy with a mixed salad.

fish main courses

Fish is always quick to cook – so what you do with it to make fabulous meals needs to be quick too! Here you can create everything from a Russian-style Salmon Coulibiac to Japanese Smoked Oyster Fishcakes with hardly any work at all. Using canned and frozen varieties means you can have these magnificent meals at your fingertips whenever the whim takes you and, as all the extras will most probably be already in your fridge, freezer or larder, that could even be tonight!

Individual seafood pies with white wine and tomatoes

This is one of my favourite recipes. The sauce ingredients are just cooked together for a few minutes, then the fish added and quickly cooked through. The mixture is spooned on to plates and topped with crisp, golden folds of filo pastry that have simply been crumpled and baked in the oven.

SERVES 6

1 x 400 g/14 oz/large can of chopped tomatoes with garlic and basil

150 ml/¹/₄ pt/²/₃ cup dry white wine

30 ml/2 tbsp tomato purée (paste)

2.5 ml/¹/₂ tsp caster (superfine) sugar

3 frozen cod steaks, cut into dice

100 g/4 oz whole baby button mushrooms or a 300 g/11 oz/medium can, drained

450 g/1 lb frozen raw seafood cocktail, thawed and thoroughly drained

150 ml/¹/₄ pt/²/₃ cup crème fraîche

Salt and freshly ground black pepper

6 sheets of filo pastry (paste)

A little olive oil

A little dried parsley, for dusting

TO SERVE
Baby new potatoes and mangetout (snow peas)

1 Put the tomatoes, wine, tomato purée and sugar in a saucepan. Bring to the boil and boil for about 5 minutes, stirring occasionally, until thick and pulpy.

2 Add the cod, mushrooms and seafood, cover and simmer gently for 4 minutes. Gently stir in the crème fraîche and season with salt and pepper.

3 Meanwhile, preheat the oven to 190°C/375°F/gas 5/fan oven 170°C. Brush the sheets of filo pastry with oil and gently scrunch each sheet to resemble pieces of crumpled paper. Place on an oiled baking (cookie) sheet and bake in the oven for about 5 minutes until crisp and golden.

4 Spoon the seafood mixture into the centre of six warm plates. Top each with a crisp crumpled filo sheet. Dust the edges of the plates with parsley and serve with baby new potatoes and mangetout.

Cod and bacon kebabs with rosemary dressing

The rectangular frozen cod portions are ideal for this as they cut into perfect cubes for threading. Just let them defrost slightly for a few minutes to make them easier to cut – they don't have to be thawed completely. The Garlic and Herb French Fries add an exciting dimension with hardly any work at all. See photograph opposite page 49.

SERVES 4

4 frozen cod portions

15 ml/1 tbsp olive oil

Salt and freshly ground black pepper

8 smoked streaky bacon rashers (slices), rinded

1 small ready-to-cook garlic baguette

FOR THE DRESSING

5 ml/1 tsp dried rosemary, crushed

90 ml/6 tbsp bottled honey and mustard dressing

15 ml/1 tbsp bottled lemon juice

15 ml/1 tbsp mayonnaise

1x 125 g/4½ oz bag of mixed salad leaves

12 cherry tomatoes, halved

Lemon wedges, to garnish (optional)

TO SERVE

Garlic and Herb French Fries (see page 91),

1 Cut each cod portion into six cubes. Toss in the oil, seasoned with a little salt and pepper.

2 Stretch the bacon rashers with the back of a knife and cut each into three equal pieces.

3 Separate the garlic bread into the slices. Discard the ends, then cut the other slices into bite-sized chunks to make 24 in all.

4 Thread a cube of cod, then a slice of bacon folded concertina-fashion, then a cube of bread on to a skewer, then repeat the threading. Make seven more kebabs in the same way.

5 Preheat the grill (broiler). Turn the grill rack over, so the kebabs will be lower under the grill. Lay the kebabs on foil on the rack. Cook under a moderate grill for about 6 minutes, turning once until golden and cooked through.

6 Meanwhile, whisk together the dressing ingredients.

7 Add a little dressing to the salad leaves, toss and pile on to four serving plates. Scatter the tomatoes around.

8 Lay two kebabs on top of each salad and spoon the remaining dressing over. Garnish with wedges of lemon, if using, and serve with Garlic and Herb French Fries.

Salmon and broccoli puff quiches

When prepared in this way, canned salmon tastes like its fresh counterpart and makes this a delightfully tasty dish. The finished quiches look extremely sophisticated too. The cutting of the pastry takes a little time but it's worth it – after all, the filling doesn't take any work at all!

SERVES 6

450 g/1 lb frozen puff pastry (paste), thawed

225 g/8 oz frozen broccoli florets, thawed

1 x 418 g/14½ oz/large can of pink or red salmon, drained

2 eggs

10 ml/2 tsp dried dill (dill weed)

200 ml/7 fl oz/scant 1 cup crème fraîche

175 ml/6 fl oz/¾ cup milk

Salt and freshly ground black pepper

90 ml/6 tbsp grated Parmesan cheese

Lemon wedges and sprigs of parsley, to garnish

1 Cut the pastry into six equal rectangles. Roll out each one thinly to 13 x 15 cm/5 x 6 in. Score a line in the pastry about 2 cm/¾ in from the outer edge all round to form the rim of each tartlet but don't cut right through. Place on two dampened baking (cookie) sheets. Leave to rest for 30 minutes.

2 Meanwhile, cut the broccoli into tiny florets and dry them on kitchen paper (paper towels).

3 Remove the skin from the salmon. Remove the bones, if you prefer, but they are very good for you (I do remove them but often eat them while I am preparing the dish!). Break the fish into bite-sized chunks with a fork.

4 Preheat the oven to 220°C/425°F/gas 7/fan oven 200°C. Beat the eggs and brush round the rims of the pastry rectangles. Bake the pastry shells in the oven for 15 minutes until risen and lightly golden. Remove from the oven and gently press down the centres to form cases. Turn the oven down to 190°C/375°F/gas 5/fan oven 170°C.

5 Arrange the broccoli and salmon in the cases and sprinkle with the dill. Whisk the crème fraîche into the remaining beaten egg with the milk and season with salt and pepper. Pour into the cases and sprinkle with the Parmesan.

6 Return the quiches to the oven and bake for about 30 minutes until set and golden. Cover very loosely with foil if over-browning.

7 Transfer the quiches to warm plates. Garnish each plate with a wedge of lemon and a sprig of parsley and serve warm.

Vermicelli with fennel and clams

The original version of this recipe usually involves cooking wine until it is reduced, then adding all sorts of ingredients, taking time and quite a lot of effort. Here it's just the wine sauce and clams – with the delicious addition of a little fresh fennel to add a touch of luxury.

SERVES 4–6

2 x 295 g/10½ oz/medium cans of baby clams

1 garlic clove, crushed, or 2.5 ml/½ tsp garlic purée (paste)

1 head of fennel, finely chopped, reserving the green fronds

1 x 295 g/10½ oz/medium can of white wine and cream sauce

Freshly ground black pepper

350 g/12 oz vermicelli

1 Drain the liquor from one of the cans of clams into a measuring jug. Make up to 250 ml/8 fl oz/1 cup with water. Drain the other can of clams, discarding the liquor.

2 Put the garlic and fennel in a saucepan with the clam juice and water. Bring to the boil and boil, stirring occasionally, for 5 minutes until the fennel is cooked and the liquor is reduced.

3 Add the wine sauce and simmer for 2 minutes, stirring. Add the clams and heat through for 2 minutes. Season with pepper.

4 Meanwhile, cook the vermicelli according to the packet directions. Drain and return to the pan. Chop the fennel fronds. Add the sauce to the pasta and toss well. Pile on to warm plates and sprinkle with the chopped fronds.

Seafood pasta layer with spinach and blue cheese

Chopped spinach and mixed seafood in a rich tomato sauce, layered with tender sheets of green lasagne and topped with a creamy blue cheese and celery sauce – delicious! This dish should be difficult to make, but it's just a few cans, cleverly combined to make a mouth-watering meal with no effort at all.

SERVES 4–6

1 x 400 g/14 oz/large can of chopped tomatoes

2.5 ml/½ tsp dried basil

1 small garlic clove, crushed, or 2.5 ml/½ tsp garlic purée (paste)

100 g/4 oz button mushrooms, sliced, or a 300 g/11 oz/medium can, drained

1 x 185 g/6½ oz/small can of tuna

1 x 170 g/6 oz/small can of prawns (shrimp), drained

1 x 250 g/9 oz/medium can of mussels in brine, drained

Salt and freshly ground black pepper

250 g/9 oz frozen chopped spinach, thawed

9 sheets of no-need-to-precook green lasagne

1 x 295 g/10½ oz/medium can of condensed celery soup

200 ml/7 fl oz/scant 1 cup crème fraîche

50 g/2 oz/½ cup crumbled soft blue cheese such as Dolcelatte

TO SERVE
A green salad

1 Put the tomatoes, basil, garlic and mushrooms in a saucepan. Bring to the boil and boil for 3 minutes until pulpy. Drain the tuna and stir in with the prawns and mussels and season lightly with salt and pepper.

2 Tip the thawed spinach into a colander and press out as much moisture as possible.

3 Spread a little of the seafood mixture in the base of a large rectangular shallow dish. Top with three sheets of lasagne, breaking the third to fit, if necessary. Spread with half the spinach, then half the remaining seafood mixture. Top with more sheets of lasagne, then the remaining spinach and seafood. Finish with a layer of lasagne.

4 Beat the soup with the crème fraîche and cheese. Spoon over the lasagne. Bake in a preheated oven at 190°C/375°F/gas 5/fan 170°C for 40 minutes until golden and cooked through. Serve hot with a green salad.

Salmon coulibiac

The original version of this Russian fish pie takes a lot of preparation when made from scratch using fresh fish and rice. Using canned fish and sweetcorn takes away all the effort but still makes an exceedingly good pie to serve to the family or a group of friends for supper.

SERVES 4

15 g/¹/₂ oz/1 tbsp butter or margarine

1 onion, chopped

200 g/7 oz/1 small can of pink or red salmon, drained

200 g/7 oz/1 small can of sweetcorn with peppers (corn with bell peppers)

45 ml/3 tbsp mayonnaise

15 ml/1 tbsp chopped fresh or frozen parsley

Salt and freshly ground black pepper

1 sheet of ready-rolled frozen puff pastry (paste), just thawed

1 egg, beaten

10 ml/2 tsp fennel, caraway or poppy seeds

Watercress, to garnish

TO SERVE
New potatoes and a cucumber salad

1 Melt the butter or margarine in a pan, add the onion and fry (sauté), stirring, for 3 minutes until softened and lightly golden. Remove from the heat.

2 Remove the skin from the salmon. Remove the bones, if you prefer, but they are very good for you. Break the fish into bite-sized chunks with a fork. Stir the sweetcorn, mayonnaise, parsley and a little salt and pepper into the onion. Fold in the salmon, taking care not to break it up completely.

3 Unroll the pastry on to a dampened baking (cookie) sheet. Spoon the filling down the centre not quite to each end. Brush the edges with beaten egg.

4 Make a series of diagonal slits in the pastry at 2 cm/³/₄ in intervals down both sides of the filling.

5 Fold the pastry ends over the filling, then lift the strips up over the filling from alternate sides to form a plait.

6 Brush with a little beaten egg to glaze, then sprinkle with the seeds.

7 Bake in a preheated oven at 220°C/425°F/gas 7/fan oven 190°C for about 25 minutes until puffy and golden brown.

8 Transfer to a serving plate and garnish with watercress. Serve warm, cut into thick slices, with new potatoes and a cucumber salad.

Sautéed cod and potatoes with anchovy olive dressing

You can, of course, use scrubbed new potatoes and fresh green beans for this recipe instead of the cans if you prefer. Simply boil the potatoes in lightly salted water for about 15 minutes or until tender, adding the beans after 10 minutes' cooking. Either way, the results will be simple and stylish.

SERVES 4

1 x 50 g/2 oz/small can of anchovies, drained

8 stoned (pitted) black olives

1 garlic clove, or 5 ml/1 tsp garlic purée (paste) (optional)

15 ml/1 tbsp pickled capers

A good handful of fresh parsley

5 ml/1 tsp bottled lemon juice

A good pinch of caster (superfine) sugar

120 ml/4 fl oz/½ cup olive oil, plus extra for frying

Salt and freshly ground black pepper

2 x 550 g/18 oz/large cans of new potatoes in their skins, halved

1 x 350 g/12 oz/medium can of whole green beans, drained and halved

4 frozen cod portions, cut into bite-sized cubes

45 ml/3 tbsp plain (all-purpose) flour

A little chopped fresh or dried parsley, to garnish

1 Rinse the anchovies with cold water, then tip into a blender or food processor. Add the olives, garlic, if using, capers, parsley, lemon and sugar. Run the machine until blended, scraping down the sides if necessary. Gradually trickle in the oil with the machine running to form a smooth dressing. Season with lots of pepper and add a dash more lemon and sugar, if liked.

2 Empty the potatoes into a pan, add the drained beans and heat through.

3 Toss the cod cubes in the flour, seasoned with a little salt and pepper.

4 Heat enough olive oil to cover the base of a frying pan (skillet). Add the cod and fry (sauté) for about 3 minutes, turning occasionally, until golden brown and cooked through. Drain on kitchen paper (paper towels).

5 Drain the potatoes and beans and return to the pan. Add half the dressing and toss. Pile on to warm serving plates and scatter the cod cubes over.

6 Trickle the remaining anchovy dressing over and sprinkle with parsley.

Japanese smoked oyster fishcakes

This is so easy, yet so impressive. If you have time, it's worth cooking round-grain rice rather than using leftover cooked long-grain as the texture is much better. I like these served with a salad made from a pack of fresh ready-prepared stir-fry vegetables with beansprouts, tossed in a little French dressing with a dash of soy sauce.

SERVES 4

100 g/4 oz/¹/₂ cup round-grain (pudding) rice

1 x 85 g/3¹/₂ oz/small can of smoked oysters, drained

1 x 85 g/3¹/₂ oz/very small can of tuna, drained

1 bunch of spring onions (scallions)

15 ml/1 tbsp soy sauce

A good pinch of ground ginger

Freshly ground black pepper

1 egg, beaten

Sunflower oil for shallow-frying

¹/₂ bottle of hoi sin sauce

1 Cook the rice in plenty of boiling lightly salted water for 20 minutes or until tender. Drain, rinse with cold water and drain again.

2 Mash the oysters and tuna in a bowl with a fork. Add the rice and mix well.

3 Trim the spring onions. Chop two and add to the fish mixture. Cut the remainder into thin shreds.

4 Add the soy sauce, ginger, some pepper and the egg to the fish mixture and mix thoroughly.

5 Heat enough oil to cover the base of a large frying pan (skillet). Shape the mixture into eight small cakes. Fry (sauté) for 2–3 minutes until golden underneath. Turn them over and brown the other sides for a further 2–3 minutes. Drain on kitchen paper (paper towels).

6 Arrange the fish cakes on warm plates with a little pile of shredded spring onion and serve with the hoi sin sauce.

Fast prawn and cheese bake with almond rice

This mixture sounds extraordinary but is truly delicious; do give it a try as I'm sure you will be pleasantly surprised. You can simply throw the ingredients together to create an extremely civilised supper that can be ready in only half an hour. If you have large appetites, use a 680 g/1½ lb bag of rice.

SERVES 4

400 g/14 oz frozen cooked, peeled prawns (shrimp), thawed and drained

1 x 295 g/10½ oz/medium can of condensed cream of mushroom soup

30 ml/2 tbsp tomato and Worcestershire table sauce

A few drops of Tabasco sauce

15 ml/1 tbsp chopped fresh or frozen parsley

50 g/2 oz/1 cup cornflakes, crushed

100 g/4 oz/1 cup grated Cheddar cheese

1 x 350 g/12 oz packet of frozen vegetable rice

15 g/½ oz/1 tbsp butter

15 ml/1 tbsp sunflower oil

50 g/2 oz/½ cup flaked (slivered) almonds

1 Preheat the oven to 200°C/400°F/gas 6/fan oven 180°C. Mix the prawns with the soup, tomato and Worcestershire sauce, the Tabasco, parsley and half the cornflakes and cheese in an ovenproof dish.

2 Mix together the remaining cornflakes and cheese and sprinkle over the top.

3 Bake in the oven for 25–30 minutes until golden and bubbling.

4 Meanwhile, cook the rice according to the packet directions. Drain.

5 Heat the butter and oil in the rinsed-out saucepan. Add the almonds and fry, stirring, until golden.

6 Return the rice to the pan and toss well. Pile on to warm serving plates and spoon the prawn mixture to one side.

Light and cool salmon mousse

This is as good as any salmon mousse I've made with fresh fish but takes just minutes to prepare. Impress your friends at a buffet party or make this your main course on a warm summer's day. It's also good as a starter for eight to ten people. If you prefer, set the mousse in an attractive serving dish rather than a mould.

SERVES 6

1 x 425 g/15 oz/large can of pink salmon, drained

1 sachet of powdered gelatine

30 ml/2 tbsp water

45 ml/3 tbsp mayonnaise

15 ml/1 tbsp tomato purée (paste)

10 ml/2 tsp anchovy essence (extract) (optional)

30 ml/2 tbsp lemon juice

Salt and freshly ground black pepper

300 ml/½ pt/1¼ cups double (heavy) or whipping cream

A little oil for greasing

½ cucumber, thinly sliced

TO SERVE
A mixed salad and baby jacket potatoes

1 Mash the fish well, discarding any skin and removing the bones if you prefer, but they are very good for you.

2 Sprinkle the gelatine over the water in a small bowl. Either place the bowl in a pan of gently simmering water or heat it briefly in the microwave until the gelatine is completely dissolved. Do not allow to boil.

3 Add the mayonnaise, tomato purée, anchovy essence (if using) and lemon juice to the fish. Mix thoroughly and season to taste. Stir in the gelatine.

4 Whip the cream until softly peaking and gently fold into the fish mixture.

5 Lightly oil a fish or jelly mould. Spoon in the mousse and level the surface. Chill until set.

6 Loosen the edges of the mousse and turn out on to a serving dish. Completely surround with overlapping thin slices of cucumber. Serve with a mixed salad and baby jacket potatoes.

Smoked mackerel and roasted beetroot salad

Mackerel and beetroot have long been favourite companions in Nordic culinary circles. Here they make a delicious and unusual warm salad, bathed in a creamy horseradish dressing. Make sure you buy the vacuum-packed beetroot that is not in vinegar or you won't get the right result.

SERVES 4

4 vacuum-packed cooked beetroot (red beets) (not in vinegar)

4 garlic cloves, peeled

45 ml/3 tbsp olive oil

Salt and freshly ground black pepper

4 smoked mackerel fillets

60 ml/4 tbsp French dressing

15 ml/1 tbsp bottled lemon juice

15 ml/1 tbsp horseradish relish

15 ml/1 tbsp mayonnaise

1 large bag of mixed salad leaves with herbs

TO SERVE
Crusty bread and unsalted (sweet) butter

1 Quarter the beetroot and place in a roasting tin (pan). Quarter the garlic lengthways and add to the beetroot. Trickle the oil all over and season with salt and pepper.

2 Roast towards the top of a preheated oven at 200°C/400°F/gas 6/fan oven 180°C for 20 minutes.

3 Meanwhile, remove the skin from the fish and cut into large chunks. Add to the beetroot for the last 5 minutes' cooking time.

4 Whisk together the remaining ingredients except the salad leaves. Add about a third to the leaves and toss, then pile them on to plates.

5 Scatter the beetroot, garlic and fish over and drizzle with the remaining dressing.

Plaice rolls with pesto and mascarpone

This dish has more than a touch of Mediterranean influence, with those favourite ingredients pesto, tomato and beautiful creamy Mascarpone cheese. As an alternative, try it with beaten out chicken or turkey breast steaks too, but use chicken stock and cook for 20–30 minutes.

SERVES 4

350 g/12 oz tagliatelle

4 large plaice fillets, skinned if black-skinned

30 ml/2 tbsp pesto from a jar

100 g/4 oz/½ cup Mascarpone cheese

Freshly ground black pepper

150 ml/¼ pt/⅔ cup fish stock, made with ½ stock cube

300 ml/½ pt/1¼ cups passata (sieved tomatoes)

A good pinch of caster (superfine) sugar

1 Cook the tagliatelle according to the packet directions. Drain and return to the pan.

2 Meanwhile, put the fish skin- or skinned-sides up on a board. Cut in halves lengthways.

3 Spread each half fillet with pesto, then Mascarpone cheese and sprinkle with pepper.

4 Roll up and place in a frying pan (skillet). Pour the fish stock around. Bring to the boil, then turn down the heat until gently bubbling around the edges. Cover with foil or a lid and cook for about 4–5 minutes until cooked through.

5 Add the passata to the tagliatelle with the sugar and a good grinding of pepper. Heat, tossing, until well blended and hot through.

6 Pile the pasta on to warm plates. Top with the fish and spoon the pan juices over.

Tuna mornay

Tender chunks of tuna blended with crunchy peanuts, bathed in a cheese and crème fraîche sauce, then baked until golden. You could use the quick cheese sauce on page 135 instead of this crème fraîche one, if you prefer. If you are allergic to nuts, simply omit them or substitute two finely chopped celery sticks for their crunch.

SERVES 4

1 x 400 g/14 oz/large can of tuna chunks, drained

100 g/4 oz/1 cup roasted peanuts

150 ml/¼ pt/⅔ cup crème fraîche

150 ml/¼ pt/⅔ cup milk

2 eggs, beaten

Freshly ground black pepper

5 ml/1 tsp dried mixed herbs

100 g/4 oz/1 cup grated Cheddar cheese

A little chopped fresh or dried parsley, to garnish

TO SERVE

A crisp green salad and crusty bread

1 Empty the tuna into a shallow ovenproof dish. Break up slightly with a fork. Scatter the nuts over.

2 Beat together the crème fraîche, milk and eggs with some black pepper, the dried mixed herbs and half the cheese. Spoon the mixture over the tuna and peanuts.

3 Sprinkle the remaining cheese liberally over the surface.

4 Bake in a preheated oven at 190°C/375°F/gas 5/fan oven 170°C for about 30 minutes until just set, golden and bubbling.

5 Sprinkle with the chopped parsley and serve hot with a crisp green salad and some crusty bread.

Brandade de morue

This classic Provençal dish is traditionally made with salt cod, soaked for 24 hours, cooked for an hour, then pounded to a paste. I use undyed smoked cod simply mashed with a few simple ingredients; the result tastes superb. Try it in small pots as an appetiser for six to eight people too, with Melba Toast (see page 127).

SERVES 4

1 large potato, peeled and cut into small chunks

250 g/9 oz undyed smoked cod

1 large garlic clove, chopped, or 5 ml/1 tsp garlic purée (paste)

1 bay leaf

60 ml/4 tbsp double (heavy) cream

15 ml/1 tbsp bottled lemon juice

30 ml/2 tbsp grated Parmesan cheese

1.5 ml/¼ tsp cayenne

5 ml/1 tsp dried chives

Salt and freshly ground black pepper

A good knob of unsalted (sweet) butter

TO SERVE
A mixed salad and coarse rustic bread

1 Boil the potato in water for 3 minutes. Add the fish, garlic and bay leaf, cover and boil for a further 5 minutes until the fish and potatoes are tender.

2 Drain off the water and discard the bay leaf. Lift the fish out of the pan and remove the skin.

3 Return the fish to the pan and add the cream, lemon juice, Parmesan, cayenne and chives. Mash with a potato masher, then beat well until the mixture forms a coarse paste.

4 Season to taste with salt and pepper, then spoon into four individual flameproof dishes. Dot with the unsalted butter.

5 Flash under a preheated grill (broiler) until the butter has melted and the top is sizzling. Serve with a mixed salad and coarse rustic bread.

Crab thermidor

A classic that normally takes ages – because you have to dress the crabs before you can even start to make the recipe! Canned crabmeat is exceptionally good and makes a quick and utterly delicious alternative. You could also cook this in ramekin dishes as a starter for six people.

SERVES 4

20 g/³/₄ oz/3 tbsp plain (all-purpose) flour

250 ml/8 fl oz/1 cup milk

50 g/2 oz/¹/₄ cup butter or margarine

Salt and freshly ground black pepper

1 bay leaf

1 x 40 g/1¹/₂ oz/small can of dressed crab

15 ml/1 tbsp brandy

5 ml/1 tsp Dijon mustard

2.5 ml/¹/₂ tsp herbes de Provence

2 x 170 g/6 oz/small cans of white crabmeat, drained

50 g/2 oz/1 cup fresh breadcrumbs

50 g/2 oz/¹/₂ cup grated Cheddar cheese

Small sprigs of parsley, to garnish

TO SERVE

New potatoes and a crisp green salad

1 Put the flour in a small saucepan. Whisk in the milk with a wire whisk until smooth. Add half the butter or margarine, a pinch of salt, a good grinding of pepper and the bay leaf. Bring to the boil and cook for 3 minutes, whisking all the time, until thick.

2 Discard the bay leaf. Whisk in the can of dressed crab, the brandy, mustard and herbs. Taste and re-season if necessary.

3 Preheat the oven to 190°C/375°F/gas 5/fan oven 170°C. Spoon a layer of half the sauce in the base of four individual shallow ovenproof dishes. Top with the white crabmeat, then the remaining sauce.

4 Melt the remaining butter or margarine and stir in the breadcrumbs, then the cheese. Spoon on top of the sauce and press down lightly. Place the dishes on a baking (cookie) sheet and bake in the oven for about 25 minutes until golden and bubbling.

5 Garnish each with a small sprig of parsley and serve hot with new potatoes and a crisp green salad.

vegetarian main courses

Whether you are vegetarian, are having vegetarian friends to dinner or simply don't fancy meat, poultry or fish sometimes, here is a selection of utterly delicious main courses for you to enjoy. They all use simple ingredients including cans, packets and other convenience foods combined with some fresh vegetables and salads to make easy, elegant meals in no time at all. Make sure any cheeses you use are suitable for vegetarians, if true veggies are eating the meals!

Wild mushroom risotto with parmesan wafers

Using a packet of mushroom risotto mix ensures a creamy, authentic texture, and adding the little extras means the flavour is fantastic too! Parmesan wafers bring a gourmet touch, but do use fresh grated Parmesan (you can buy it ready grated), not the sort sold in tubs, which is dried so won't melt. See photograph opposite page 96.

SERVES 4–6

FOR THE PARMESAN WAFERS
100 g/4 oz /1 cup freshly grated Parmesan cheese

FOR THE RISOTTO
1 x 250 g/9 oz packet of mushroom risotto mix

100 g/4 oz mixed mushrooms, sliced

15 g/½ oz/1 tbsp butter or margarine, plus extra for greasing

60 ml/4 tbsp double (heavy) cream

Freshly ground black pepper

A little chopped fresh or dried parsley, to garnish

TO SERVE
A crisp green salad

1 Put 12 spoonfuls of Parmesan cheese well apart on a greased baking (cookie) sheet. Flatten slightly. Bake in a preheated oven at 200°C/400°F/gas 6/fan oven 180°C for 10 minutes until melted. Remove from the oven, leave to cool slightly, then transfer to a wire rack to cool completely.

2 Make up the risotto mix according to the packet directions. While it is cooking, stew the mixed sliced mushrooms in the butter or margarine, stirring occasionally, for 5 minutes.

3 When the risotto is just cooked, stir in the mushrooms and their juices and the cream. Season with pepper.

4 Spoon into warm shallow bowls or deep plates and garnish with parsley. Serve with the Parmesan wafers and a crisp green salad.

Ratatouille and cheese dolmas on garlic chick peas

If you had to start by making the ratatouille you would be embarking on a very time-consuming dish. However, cheating and using canned ratatouille works a dream and the flavour is extremely moreish. The whole effect is very Mediterranean and everyone will be sure to enjoy it.

SERVES 4

8 large cabbage leaves

1 x 425 g/15 oz/large can of ratatouille

30 ml/2 tbsp long-grain rice

2.5 ml/½ tsp dried basil

50 g/2 oz/½ cup finely diced Cheddar cheese

300 ml/½ pt/1¼ cups vegetable stock, made with 1 stock cube

30 ml/2 tbsp tomato purée (paste)

Salt and freshly ground black pepper

1 large garlic clove, crushed, or 5 ml/1 tsp garlic purée (paste)

30 ml/2 tbsp olive oil

1 x 425 g/15 oz/large can of chick peas (garbanzos), drained

50 g/2 oz/½ cup sliced black olives

30 ml/2 tbsp chopped fresh or frozen parsley

1 Cut out and discard the thick central base stalk from the cabbage leaves. Cook the leaves in boiling water for 2 minutes. Drain, rinse with cold water and drain again. Dry on kitchen paper (paper towels).

2 Mix the ratatouille with the rice, basil and Cheddar.

3 Lay the leaves upside-down on a board and overlap the two points where the stalks were. Spoon the ratatouille mixture on top. Fold in the sides, then roll up. Pack into a heavy-based flameproof casserole dish (Dutch oven).

4 Mix the stock with the tomato purée, season to taste and pour over. Bring to the boil, reduce the heat, cover and cook gently for 30 minutes until the cabbage and rice are tender.

5 Meanwhile, cook the garlic gently in the oil for 1 minute without browning. Add the chick peas and crush with a fork. Stir in the olives and parsley and season to taste. Heat through, stirring.

6 Pile the crushed chickpeas on to warm plates and arrange the dolmas alongside. Spoon the juices over and serve.

Falafel with minted cucumber salsa

Traditionally falafel are made by soaking dried chickpeas, then boiling them for ages, then mashing them and mixing them, and finally frying them. Here the process takes just a few minutes to prepare and cook – including making a fresh salsa to serve with them. Brilliant!

SERVES 4

FOR THE FALAFEL

1 x 425 g/15 oz/large can of chickpeas (garbanzos) drained

1 small onion

1 small garlic clove or 2.5 ml/½ tsp garlic purée (paste)

1.5 ml/¼ tsp dried chilli flakes

5 ml/1 tsp ground cumin

5 ml/1 tsp ground coriander (cilantro)

5 ml/1 tsp dried parsley

Salt and freshly ground black pepper

15 ml/1 tbsp potato flour

40 g/1½ oz/⅓ cup plain (all-purpose) flour

60 ml/4 tbsp milk

Oil for deep-frying

FOR THE SALSA

¼ cucumber, finely chopped

2 spring onions (scallions), finely chopped

15 ml/1 tbsp bottled mint sauce

A good pinch of caster (superfine) sugar

75 ml/5 tbsp plain yoghurt

TO SERVE

Pitta breads and a mixed salad

1 To make the falafel, put all the ingredients except the flour and milk in a blender or food processor and purée to a coarse paste.

2 Shape the mixture into 20 small balls. Roll in the flour, then in the milk, then the flour again. Chill for at least 30 minutes.

3 To make the salsa, mix together all the ingredients and season to taste. Chill until ready to serve.

4 Deep-fry the falafel a few at a time for 3 minutes until golden. Drain on kitchen paper (paper towels).

5 Serve with the salsa, pitta breads and a mixed salad.

Velvet macaroni cheese with tomato topping

This is a traditional and popular family dish, but you normally have to make a cheese sauce to add to the pasta – which takes effort and two dirty pans. Here you just throw in the cheesy ingredients after cooking the pasta and the result is a smooth, creamy, very rich dish, perfect for lunch or supper in a hurry.

SERVES 4

225 g/8 oz short-cut macaroni

200 g/7 oz/scant 1 cup cheese spread

60 ml/4 tbsp milk

Salt and freshly ground black pepper

4–6 tomatoes, sliced

TO SERVE

Ciabatta bread and a crisp green salad

1 Cook the pasta according to the packet directions. Drain and return to the pan.

2 Stir in the cheese spread and milk. Season to taste. Heat through, stirring.

3 Spoon the mixture into one large or four small flameproof dishes.

4 Arrange the tomato slices over the surface. Cook under a preheated grill (broiler) until the tomatoes are cooked and lightly browning round the edges.

5 Serve with ciabatta bread and a crisp green salad.

Gnocchi with creamy dolcelatte and celery sauce

Making gnocchi from scratch is such a fiddle and I just can't see the point when the vacuum packs of ready made are so good. The important thing is that the sauce is very good and very easy. Here I've mixed blue cheese and crème fraîche with some chopped celery and onion for a simple but delicious combination.

SERVES 4–6

2 vacuum packs of ready-made gnocchi

3 celery sticks, chopped

1 onion, chopped

15 g/½ oz/1 tbsp butter or margarine

450 ml/¾ pt/2 cups crème fraîche

175 g/6 oz/1½ cups crumbled Dolcelatte cheese

25 g/1 oz/¼ cup grated Parmesan cheese

10 ml/2 tsp dried chives

Freshly ground black pepper

Tiny sprigs of fresh basil or a few extra dried chives, to garnish

TO SERVE
Crusty bread and a tomato salad

1 Cook the gnocchi according to the packet directions. Transfer to one large or four to six small serving dishes.

2 Meanwhile, gently cook the celery and onion in the butter or margarine for 2 minutes, stirring, to soften. Remove from the heat and stir in the crème fraîche, cheeses and chives. Add a good grinding of black pepper.

3 Spoon the sauce over the gnocchi. Bake in a preheated oven at 200°C/400°F/gas 6/fan oven 180°C for about 25 minutes until golden and bubbling.

4 Garnish with tiny sprigs of basil or a sprinkling of dried chives. Serve with crusty bread and a tomato salad.

Spinach and tagliatelle bake with glazed tomatoes

Creamed spinach makes a perfect sauce for pasta, with the addition of a few extra flavourings to make the texture and flavour truly delicious. The glazed vine tomatoes add an elegant touch and are so easy to prepare. They are worth the little extra cost as they have such a wonderful flavour.

SERVES 4

350 g/12 oz tagliatelle

1 large onion, chopped

1 large garlic clove, crushed, or 5 ml/1 tsp garlic purée (paste)

75 g/3 oz/⅓ cup butter or margarine

1 x 450 g/1 lb packet of frozen creamed spinach, thawed

Salt and freshly ground black pepper

A good pinch of grated nutmeg

4 sprigs of small tomatoes on the vine (3–4 on each sprig)

30 ml/2 tbsp olive oil

30 ml/2 tbsp balsamic vinegar

5 ml/1 tsp caster (superfine) sugar

1 Cook the tagliatelle in boiling, lightly salted water in a flameproof casserole dish (Dutch oven) for 8 minutes until almost tender but still slightly 'nutty'. Drain thoroughly in a colander.

2 Fry (sauté) the onion and garlic in the casserole dish in 50 g/2 oz/¼ cup of the butter or margarine for 2 minutes, stirring, until lightly golden.

3 Return the pasta to the pan and toss gently. Add the creamed spinach and toss again. Season to taste and add the nutmeg. Toss again.

4 Dot with the remaining butter or margarine. Bake in a preheated oven at 190°C/375°F/gas 5/fan oven 170°C for 30 minutes until hot through and lightly golden on top.

5 Meanwhile, lay the tomatoes in a shallow baking dish. Trickle with the oil and turn over gently to coat completely. Sprinkle all over with the balsamic vinegar, then the sugar and a little salt and pepper. Place in the oven with the tagliatelle half way through cooking (they will take about 15 minutes in all).

6 Spoon the pasta mixture on to four warm plates. Lay a sprig of cooked tomatoes to one side and spoon any juices over. Serve hot.

Baked tofu and egg madras

Nothing could be simpler than this delicious dish and the result is truly sensational! Use microwave rice if you're not too great with boiling it from scratch or for a completely hassle-free meal. Or you could use boil-in-the-bag rice, which is also simple and foolproof.

SERVES 4

1 x 250 g/9 oz block of firm tofu, cubed

1 x 425 g/15 oz jar of Madras curry sauce

8 eggs

30 ml/2 tbsp chopped fresh coriander (cilantro)

TO SERVE
Plain basmati rice

1 Preheat the oven to 180°C/350°F/gas 4/fan oven 160°C.

2 Put the cubes of tofu in four individual ovenproof serving dishes. Spoon the sauce over. Cover the dishes with foil and bake in the oven for 5 minutes to heat through.

3 Carefully remove the foil. Stir gently, then make two hollows in each dish and break an egg into each hollow (two per dish). Sprinkle with the coriander and re-cover with the foil. Return to the oven for 10–15 minutes until the eggs are cooked to your liking.

4 Serve with plain basmati rice.

Vegetable and lentil stir-fry with black bean sauce

Almost instant noodles mixed with canned pulses – so no soaking or boiling – and the easiest of sauce mixtures all from storecupboard ingredients makes a surprisingly delicious dish. The chopped spring onions add a touch of elegance but you could just sprinkle the dish with dried chives if you don't have any.

SERVES 4

2 slabs of Chinese egg noodles

45 ml/3 tbsp sunflower oil

1 x 225 g/8 oz packet of fresh mixed stir-fry vegetables

1 x 425 g/15 oz/large can of green or brown lentils, drained

30 ml/2 tbsp bottled black bean sauce

15 ml/1 tbsp soy sauce

15 ml/1 tbsp medium dry sherry or apple juice

1 bunch of spring onions (scallions), chopped, to garnish

1 Cook the noodles according to the packet directions. Drain thoroughly.

2 Heat the oil in a large frying pan (skillet) or wok. Add the vegetables and stir-fry for 2 minutes.

3 Add the cooked noodles and lentils and toss for 1 minute.

4 Add the sauces and sherry or apple juice and toss again. Spoon into bowls and garnish with chopped spring onions.

Conchiglie alla genovese

You can use cooked leftover new potatoes and French beans if you have them. This colourful, filling meal is based on a classic Italian peasant dish and still has all the flavour but none of the effort. If you have some fresh basil, tear a few leaves and sprinkle over before serving.

SERVES 4

225 g/8 oz conchiglie (pasta shells)

1 x 300 g/11 oz/medium can of new potatoes, drained and quartered

1 x 295 g/10½ oz/medium can of cut French (green) beans, drained

15 ml/1 tbsp olive oil

12 cherry tomatoes

45 ml/3 tbsp pesto from a jar

Grated Parmesan cheese, to garnish

1 Cook the pasta according to the packet directions. Drain and return to the pan.

2 Meanwhile, put the potatoes and beans in a non-stick saucepan with the oil. Cover and cook over a very gentle heat, shaking the pan occasionally, until hot through. Add the tomatoes and heat for a further 1 minute until the tomatoes are hot but still hold their shape.

3 Add the pesto to the pasta and toss to coat. Tip the heated vegetables into the pan and toss again over a gentle heat until thoroughly mixed and piping hot. Spoon into warm bowls and sprinkle with a little grated Parmesan cheese.

Asparagus and flageolet soufflé

Don't leave soufflés to the professionals. You don't need any skill for this gloriously light and fluffy, pale green concoction! Try other mixtures such as canned sliced mushrooms and mushroom soup with brown lentils. Bake small scrubbed potatoes on the top shelf for 30 minutes before putting the soufflé in the oven to cook.

SERVES 4

Butter for greasing

1 x 410 g/14½ oz/large can of cut asparagus spears, drained

1 x 295 g/10½ oz/medium can of condensed asparagus soup

75 g/3 oz/¾ cup grated Parmesan cheese

30 ml/2 tbsp chopped fresh or frozen parsley

4 eggs, separated

1 x 300 g/11 oz/medium can of flageolet beans, drained, rinsed and drained again

Freshly ground black pepper

TO SERVE
Baby jacket potatoes and a mixed salad

1 Preheat the oven to 200°C/400°F/gas 6/fan oven 180°C. Grease a 20 cm/8 in soufflé dish and put the asparagus spears in the base.

2 Whisk the soup with the Parmesan, parsley and egg yolks. Stir in the beans.

3 Whisk the egg whites until stiff, then fold into the soup mixture with a metal spoon.

4 Turn into the prepared soufflé dish and bake in the oven for 30 minutes or until risen and a rich golden brown.

5 Serve straight away with baby jacket potatoes and a mixed salad.

Peanut and soya bean flan with tomato chilli salsa

No need to worry that you can't make pastry; this peanut one is simply mixed together with a fork – no rubbing in or rolling and folding required. The filling, too, is just a simple mix of storecupboard standbys. The golden flan is then served with a fresh salsa for added goodness and flavour.

SERVES 4–6

FOR THE PASTRY
45 ml/3 tbsp smooth peanut butter

100 g/4 oz/½ cup soft tub margarine

30 ml/2 tbsp water

225 g/8 oz/2 cups plain
(all-purpose) flour

5 ml/1 tsp salt

FOR THE FILLING
1 x 425 g/15 oz/large can of soya
beans, drained

2 spring onion (scallions), finely chopped

2 celery sticks, finely chopped

50 g/2 oz/½ cup roasted peanuts

60 ml/4 tbsp mayonnaise

Freshly ground black pepper

50 g/2 oz/½ cup grated Cheddar cheese

FOR THE SALSA
4 ripe tomatoes, chopped

75 ml/5 tbsp tomato and chilli salsa
from a jar

TO SERVE
A mixed salad

1 Preheat the oven to 200°C/400°F/gas 6/fan oven 180°C. Put all the pastry ingredients in a bowl and mix with a fork until it forms a dough. Press the dough into the base and sides of a 20 cm/8 in flan dish (pie pan). Prick the base with a fork and fill with crumpled foil.

2 Bake the pastry case (pie shell) in the oven for 10 minutes. Remove the foil and bake for a further 5 minutes to dry out.

3 Turn down the oven to 190°C/375°F/gas 5/fan oven 170°C. Mix together the filling ingredients except the cheese and spoon into the flan. Cover with the cheese and return to the oven for 25 minutes until golden and hot through.

4 Meanwhile, mix together the tomatoes and salsa and season to taste. Chill until ready to serve.

5 Serve the flan warm with the tomato chilli salsa and a mixed salad.

Onion and white bean stroganoff

You do need to peel onions for this, but they don't have to be cut up precisely, and you could use frozen chopped onions if you really can't be bothered! They are then just fried and mixed with canned beans, soured cream and some fresh parsley for a glorious taste sensation to serve with easily cooked wild rice mix.

SERVES 4

FOR THE RICE
225 g/8 oz/1 cup wild rice mix

1 vegetable stock cube

15 ml/1 tbsp pickled green peppercorns

FOR THE STROGANOFF
50 g/2 oz/¼ cup butter or margarine

4 large onions, halved and sliced

2 x 425 g/15 oz/large cans of
cannellini beans, drained

300 ml/½ pt/1¼ cups soured
(dairy sour) cream

Salt and freshly ground black pepper

A little chopped fresh or dried
parsley, to garnish

TO SERVE
A mixed salad

1 Cook the wild rice mix in plenty of boiling water with the stock cube added for 20 minutes. Drain in a colander, return to the pan and stir in the peppercorns.

2 Meanwhile, melt the butter or margarine over a gentle heat in a large saucepan. Add the onions and cook, stirring, for 3 minutes until softening but not browning. Turn down the heat to low, cover the pan and cook very gently for a further 5 minutes until soft but not brown, stirring occasionally.

3 Add the beans and soured cream and heat through. Season to taste.

4 Pile the rice on to warm plates and spoon the stroganoff to one side. Sprinkle with parsley and serve with a mixed salad.

Limoges potato pie

Traditionally you would have to fiddle around scrubbing potatoes and cutting them very thinly so they cook properly in the pie – the result can be really disappointing if they aren't cooked through! Here canned potatoes ensure a soft, creamy filling encased in golden, flaky pastry. Minimum effort but maximum flavour guaranteed!

SERVES 4–6

1 box of 2 sheets of frozen puff pastry (paste), thawed

2 x 550 g/18 oz/large cans of potatoes, drained

10 ml/2 tsp dried minced onion

1 large garlic clove, chopped, or 5 ml/1 tsp garlic purée (paste)

10 ml/2 tsp dried chives

Salt and freshly ground black pepper

50 g/2 oz/¼ cup butter or margarine

150 ml/¼ pt/⅔ cup double (heavy) or whipping cream

1 egg

TO SERVE
Pickles

1 Preheat the oven to 220°C/425°F/gas 7/fan oven 200°C. Use one sheet of pastry to line an 18 x 23 cm/7 x 9 in shallow ovenproof dish.

2 Slice the potatoes. Layer the potato slices, onion, garlic and chives, seasoning each layer with salt and pepper and dotting each layer with butter or margarine.

3 Beat together the cream and egg and pour over the potatoes, reserving about 10 ml/2 tsp for glazing.

4 Lay the remaining pastry on top, crimping the edges together between the finger and thumb. Brush the top of the pie with the reserved egg and cream to glaze. Make leaves out of the pastry trimmings and arrange on the pie. Brush the leaves with the very last of the egg and cream. Make a hole in the centre to allow steam to escape.

5 Place the pie on a baking (cookie) sheet and bake in the oven for about 35 minutes or until risen and golden and the filling is just set but still creamy.

6 Serve warm with pickles.

side dishes and snacks

Canned or frozen veggies are fine nutritionally but their texture is not always brilliant. However, with a little bit of imagination they can be turned into gourmet treats, let alone cheats! There are times, too, when you fancy a snack and would like more than a ham sandwich. Here's your chance to create mouthwatering morsels using storecupboard standbys.

Corn and chive fritters

These are the quickest, crunchiest fritters I know. Serve them on their own with some bought tartare sauce as a starter or snack or as an accompaniment to grilled or fried chicken. Use the same extra-fast batter to coat other vegetables, fruit, fish or even pieces of chicken breast before deep-frying.

SERVES 4

100 g/4 oz/1 cup self-raising (self-rising) flour

2.5 ml/½ tsp salt

150 ml/¼ pt/⅔ cup tepid water

1 x 350 g/12 oz/medium can of sweetcorn (corn), drained

10 ml/2 tsp dried chives

Oil for deep-frying

1 Sift the flour and salt in a bowl. Gradually mix in the water to form a thick batter that will drop off a spoon.

2 Stir in the corn and chives.

3 Heat the oil in a deep-fat fryer to 190°C/375°F or until a cube of day-old bread browns in 30 seconds. Drop spoonfuls of the batter into the oil and fry (sauté) for about 3 minutes, turning once or twice, until crisp and golden.

4 Drain on kitchen paper (paper towels) and serve hot.

Minted creamed peas with lettuce

This is a great way to use up the outside leaves of a lettuce. It's based on a classic French recipe but is far less complicated – in fact it isn't difficult at all. It goes well with all kinds of main dishes, especially grilled meats such as lamb chops or even good-quality sausages.

SERVES 4

225 g/8 oz/2 cups frozen peas

1 packet of onion sauce mix

Milk

A good handful of shredded lettuce

30 ml/2 tbsp double (heavy) cream

Freshly ground black pepper

1 Cook the peas either in a saucepan or in the microwave according to the packet directions. Drain.

2 Meanwhile, make up the sauce mix using 30 ml/2 tbsp less milk than recommended.

3 Stir in the peas and lettuce and simmer for 2 minutes.

4 Stir in the cream and season with pepper.

Honey-glazed carrots

This is best if you can use fresh baby carrots, but if time is really short, use canned whole baby carrots instead of fresh ones but don't cook them first. Simply heat the glaze ingredients, then toss the carrots gently in the mixture for as little time as possible as they will be very soft.

SERVES 4

1 x 350 g/12 oz pack of ready-prepared baby carrots

A good knob of butter

30 ml/2 tbsp clear honey

Salt and freshly ground black pepper

5 ml/1 tsp dried parsley

1 Cook the carrots in boiling water for 3 minutes. Drain thoroughly.

2 Melt the butter in a frying pan. Add the carrots and toss for 1 minute.

3 Add the honey and a little salt and pepper and cook, tossing frequently, for 3–5 minutes until stickily glazed and just cooked but still with some bite. Sprinkle with the dried parsley before serving.

Golden glazed potatoes

Canned potatoes are all very well but the texture and flavour aren't brilliant. However, tossed in caramelised butter, they taste completely different – especially served with roasted or grilled meats or poultry – and no one will know you haven't spent ages scraping and boiling them.

SERVES 4–6

25 g/1 oz/2 tbsp caster (superfine) sugar

50 g/2 oz/¼ cup butter

2 x 550 g/18 oz/large cans of new potatoes, drained

2.5 ml/½ tsp dried mixed herbs

Salt and freshly ground black pepper

1 Put the sugar in a large heavy-based frying pan (skillet) and heat gently, stirring occasionally, until it melts and caramelises but do not allow to burn. When golden, add the butter and stir until it melts and is blended with the caramel.

2 Add the potatoes and herbs and season well. Heat, shaking the pan occasionally, until the potatoes are hot through and glazed.

3 Spoon into a serving dish and serve hot.

Creamed potatoes

Instant potato may not be that great on its own but made like this it's the perfect fluffy, creamy mash and no one will know you haven't peeled, boiled and pulverised a mountain of potatoes! I can't give you the exact amount of water needed because it varies according to the brand of potato.

SERVES 4

300 ml/½ pt/1¼ cups whipping cream

Approximately 300 ml/½ pt/1¼ cups water

4 servings of instant mashed potato flakes

A good knob of butter

Salt and freshly ground black pepper

1 Pour the cream into a measuring jug. Make up with water to the amount of liquid required on the packet for four servings of potato (usually water or milk and water mixed). Tip into a saucepan and bring to the boil.

2 Sprinkle the instant potato over the surface and whisk in with a fork until fluffy and well blended. Beat in the butter and season with salt and pepper. If necessary, add a dash more of boiling water to give the consistency you like.

Tabbouleh without the chopping

I adore Middle Eastern tabbouleh, but although the bulgar is very easy to prepare, adding all those herbs means a lot of preparation – unless you cheat. This way you just stir in the flavour; it couldn't be simpler! It is particularly good served wrapped in lettuce leaves for a starter.

SERVES 4

100 g/4 oz/¹/₂ cup bulgar (cracked wheat)

300 ml/¹/₂ pt/1¹/₄ cups boiling water

30 ml/2 tbsp coriander (cilantro) from a jar

15 ml/1 tbsp garden mint from a jar

1 garlic clove, crushed, or 5 ml/1 tsp garlic purée (paste)

30 ml/2 tbsp chopped frozen parsley

45 ml/3 tbsp olive oil

15 ml/1 tbsp bottled lemon juice

Salt and freshly ground black pepper

1 Put the bulgar in a bowl and cover with the boiling water. Leave to soak for 30 minutes until it has absorbed all the water.

2 Stir in the remaining ingredients, sharpening with lemon juice and seasoning with salt and pepper to taste. Leave to cool, then chill. Fluff up with a fork before serving.

Chinese noodles with vegetables

When you fancy something a bit different, perhaps with some barbecued chicken or with bought Chinese ribs, this is the ideal fast and delicious accompaniment. These noodles also make a quick lunch dish, served with a handful of cashew nuts or peanuts for texture and added protein. See photograph opposite page 97.

SERVES 4

2 slabs of Chinese egg noodles

1 x 425 g/15 oz/large can of Chinese stir-fry vegetables, drained

15 ml/1 tbsp soy sauce

1 Cook the noodles according to the packet directions. Add the drained vegetables for the last minute to heat through. Drain and return to the pan.

2 Add the soy sauce, toss and serve.

Garlic and herb french fries

Oven chips are a great boon to modern cooks in a hurry – as well as containing less fat than traditional chips – but they don't really have much flavour. On their own, they can't compare with the real thing. So try my fries flavoured with herbs and garlic to make them sing!

SERVES 4–6

700 g/1½ lb bag of frozen American-style thin fries

10 ml/2 tsp dried herbes de Provence

5 ml/1 tsp garlic salt

1 Empty the frozen fries into a large baking tin (pan). Sprinkle the herbs and garlic salt over and toss with the hands to distribute evenly. Spread out well.

2 Cook according to the packet directions, tossing once or twice.

Galette lyonnaise

When you make this classic dish from scratch it can take quite a long time to peel and cook the potatoes ready to put it all together. Try my method. No one will ever guess you used instant mash instead – except no tell-tale potato peelings – as it will look and taste delicious!

SERVES 4

2 large onions, sliced

75 g/3 oz/¹⁄₃ cup butter or margarine, plus extra for greasing

100 g/4 oz instant mashed potato flakes

400 ml/14 fl oz/1¾ cups boiling water

30 ml/2 tbsp dried milk powder (non-fat dry milk)

30 ml/2 tbsp double (heavy) cream

Salt and freshly ground black pepper

1 Preheat the oven to 190°C/375°F/gas 5/fan oven 170°C. Fry (sauté) the onions in 50 g/2 oz/¹⁄₄ cup of the butter or margarine for 3–4 minutes until softened and golden.

2 Tip the potato into a bowl. Add the water and milk powder and beat until smooth. Beat in the cream and onions and season to taste.

3 Spread the mixture in a lightly greased shallow ovenproof dish. Dot with the remaining butter or margarine.

4 Bake in the oven for about 40 minutes or until golden.

Spiced tropicana salad

This is delicious served with any spicy meat, poultry or fish. I love it, too, with barbecued ribs or grilled pork chops. There's no cooking at all, you just wash and dice the ingredients for a wonderful crispy salad with a tropical fruit flavour and a hint of chilli and mixed spice to give it zing!

SERVES 4

1 x 550 g/18 oz/large can of pineapple pieces, drained

1 large green (bell) pepper, diced

1 large red or yellow pepper, diced

1 large under-ripe banana, sliced

A good pinch of chilli powder

A good pinch of mixed (apple pie) spice

60 ml/4 tbsp bottled French dressing

Lettuce leaves

1 Mix together all the ingredients except the lettuce.

2 Line individual salad bowls with lettuce leaves and spoon in the salad.

Mixed bean salad

I know this is an old favourite but it is far too good to leave out of Cheat Your Way to Gourmet Eating. *Canned pulses are a boon all the time – no long soaking and cooking and you can be sure that all the toxins in the original dried product have been removed. Keep cans in your storecupboard at all times!*

SERVES 4

1 x 425 g/15 oz/large can of mixed pulses

10 ml/2 tsp dried minced onion

1 x 200 g/7 oz/small can of pimientos, drained and diced

4 cornichons from a jar, chopped

45 ml/3 tbsp bottled French dressing

2.5 ml/¹/₂ tsp dried oregano

Salt and freshly ground black pepper

10 ml/2 tsp dried chives, to garnish

1 Drain the pulses, rinse under cold water and drain again.

2 Tip into a salad bowl. Add the remaining ingredients and toss well but gently.

3 Chill for at least 30 minutes, preferably longer, to allow the flavours to develop.

Quick smoked mackerel pâté

This will soon become one of your favourite quick starters or snacks for any occasion. It's highly nutritious, extra-easy to make and utterly delicious served either on toast, as it is here, or on crackers. You can even use it as a sandwich filling. I like vacuum-packed mackerel but use canned if you prefer.

SERVES 2–4

2 smoked mackerel fillets, skinned

60 ml/4 tbsp crème fraîche

15 ml/1 tbsp mayonnaise

2.5 ml/½ tsp dried dill (dill weed)

A few drops of bottled lemon juice

Salt and freshly ground black pepper

4 slices of bread

Butter

1 Put the mackerel fillets in a bowl and break up with a fork.

2 Beat in the crème fraîche, mayonnaise and dill. Season to taste with lemon juice, salt and pepper.

3 Toast the bread and spread with butter. Pile the pâté on top and serve.

Classy beans on toast

Yes, okay, you can always open a can of baked beans in tomato sauce but this is in a different class altogether! Soft, creamy white beans folded through a rich tomato mixture, enhanced with garlic and onion and served drizzled with olive oil. It's perfect for family meals and even good enough to serve to guests.

SERVES 2–4

1 x 225 g/8 oz/small can of chopped tomatoes

1 small garlic clove, chopped, or 2.5 ml/½ tsp garlic purée (paste)

15 ml/1 tbsp dried minced onion

1 x 425 g/15 oz/large can of cannellini beans, drained

2.5 ml/½ tsp caster (superfine) sugar

Salt and freshly ground black pepper

15 ml/1 tbsp chopped fresh or frozen parsley (optional)

4 thick slices of ciabatta (or ordinary) bread

60 ml/4 tbsp olive oil

1 Put the tomatoes in a pan with the garlic and onion. Simmer for 3 minutes, stirring, until pulpy.

2 Stir in the beans, sugar and salt and pepper to taste. Throw in the parsley, if using, and heat through.

3 Toast the bread. Place on plates and drizzle with the olive oil so it trickles on the plates as well as on the toast. Spoon the beans on top and serve.

Photograph opposite:
Wild mushroom risotto with parmesan wafers (see page 73)

Giant crostini with tapenade and anchovies

You can make tiny versions of these crostini with thin slices of French stick to serve as an appetiser with drinks if you prefer. They are simply a mixture of classic Mediterranean ingredients straight off the supermarket shelves; it's the clever combination of them that makes these snacks so special.

SERVES 4

1 small baguette, sliced lengthways into 4

Olive oil for brushing

1 x 50 g/2 oz/small can of anchovies, drained

1 x 90 g/3½ oz jar of black or green tapenade

15 ml/1 tbsp pickled capers, drained and chopped

200 g/7 oz/scant 1 cup medium-fat soft cheese

TO SERVE
Cherry tomatoes

1 Brush the baguette slices liberally with olive oil on both sides.

2 Grill (broil) on both sides until golden at the edges and soft in the middle.

3 Meanwhile, rinse the anchovies under cold running water. Reserve four fillets for garnish and finely chop the remainder. Mix into the tapenade with the capers.

4 Spread the cheese on the toasted bread, then top with the tapenade mixture and garnish each with a rolled up anchovy fillet. Serve with cherry tomatoes.

Photograph opposite:
Chinese noodles with vegetables
(see page 91)

Tomato, spinach and chicken panini

Most supermarkets have finally caught up with providing chargrill-marked panini in the bread section, so you can make your own panini as good as anything you'll find in the upmarket Mediterranean sandwich shops. You can use sandwich baguettes or large ciabatta rolls instead if you prefer.

SERVES 4

4 panini

Olive oil for brushing

120 ml/8 tbsp tomato and basil pasta sauce from a jar

4 slices of cooked chicken breast

4 handfuls of fresh baby spinach leaves

Freshly ground black pepper

1 Preheat a hinged grill, sandwich maker or grill (broiler). Split the breads not quite right through and brush inside and out with olive oil.

2 Spread inside with the tomato and basil sauce, then add the chicken and spinach. Season with pepper.

3 Cook in the hinged grill or sandwich maker for about 3 minutes or until toasted and hot through, or under a conventional grill for 2–3 minutes on each side, pressing down with a fish slice during cooking.

Tomato and mushroom croissant melt

*This is another simple favourite in my family – crisp buttery croissants filled with a
creamy mushroom mixture, sliced tomatoes and gooey cheese. It's an easy recipe to
adapt, too, so you can experiment with different kinds of cheese, pieces of bacon, or
your favourite herbs.*

SERVES 4

4 large croissants

**1 x 170 g/6 oz/small can of
creamed mushrooms**

2 tomatoes, thinly sliced

4 pinches of dried basil

**50 g/2 oz/¹/₂ cup grated Mozzarella or
Cheddar cheese**

1 Preheat the grill (broiler). Turn the grill rack upside-down.

2 Split the croissants, taking care not to cut through completely. Fill
them with the mushrooms, tomatoes, basil and cheese.

3 Grill (broil) under a moderate grill, turning once, until hot through and
the cheese has melted. Take care not to allow the croissants to burn.

The best maxi-topped stone-baked pizzas

These are so much better than bought extra-topped pizzas. The simple cheese and tomato base makes the ideal vehicle for your own creations. Make sure you buy an Italian-style stone-baked pizza as the dough is much better than other types of pizza. It's worth spending a little more for the best flavour and texture.

Spicy beef

SERVES 1–2

1 frozen stone-baked Marguerita pizza

FOR THE TOPPING
75 g/3 oz freeflow frozen minced (ground) beef

15 ml/1 tbsp dried minced onion

2.5 ml/½ tsp chilli powder

1 small red or green (bell) pepper, chopped, or 1 canned pimiento cap, chopped

15 ml/1 tbsp tomato purée (paste)

A pinch of caster (superfine) sugar

2.5 ml/½ tsp dried oregano

Salt and freshly ground black pepper

50 g/2 oz/½ cup grated Mozzarella cheese

1 Preheat the oven to 220°C/425°F/gas 7/fan oven 200°C. Put the pizza on a baking (cookie) sheet.

2 Put the beef in a small saucepan and cook, stirring, until the beef is no longer pink and all the grains are separate. Stir in the remaining ingredients except the Mozzarella, seasoning to taste. Cook for 2 minutes, stirring.

3 Spread the beef mixture over the pizza and sprinkle with the Mozzarella. Bake in the oven for about 20 minutes until cooked through and the cheese is melted, bubbling and turning lightly golden in just a few places.

Pizza a la reine

SERVES 1–2

1 frozen stone-baked Marguerita pizza

FOR THE TOPPING

6 button mushrooms, sliced

30 ml/2 tbsp olive oil

4 thin slices of pancetta or raw cured ham, cut into pieces

50 g/2 oz/½ cup grated Mozzarella cheese

2.5 ml/1½ tsp dried oregano

6 black olives

Freshly ground black pepper

1 Preheat the oven to 220°C/425°F/gas 7/fan oven 200°C. Put the pizza on a baking (cookie) sheet.

2 Cook the mushrooms in half the oil, stirring, for 2 minutes either in a small pan or in a bowl in the microwave.

3 Scatter the mushrooms and pancetta or ham over the pizza. Sprinkle with the Mozzarella and oregano, then scatter the olives on top.

4 Drizzle with the remaining oil and season with pepper. Bake in the oven for about 20 minutes until cooked through and the cheese is melted, bubbling and turning lightly golden in just a few places.

Pizza di mare

SERVES 1–2

1 frozen stone-baked Marguerita pizza

FOR THE TOPPING

100 g/4 oz/½ cup medium-fat soft cheese

1 x 185 g/6½ oz/small can of tuna, drained

100 g/4 oz frozen cooked peeled prawns (shrimp), thawed

50 g/2 oz/½ cup grated Mozzarella cheese

2.5 ml/½ tsp dried oregano

Freshly ground black pepper

15 ml/1 tbsp olive oil

A little chopped fresh or dried parsley, to garnish

1 Preheat the oven to 220°C/425°F/gas 7/fan oven 200°C. Put the pizza on a baking (cookie) sheet.

2 Put teaspoonfuls of the soft cheese over the pizza. Break up the tuna into small pieces and scatter over the pizza. Drain the prawns on kitchen paper (paper towels), then scatter over.

3 Sprinkle with the Mozzarella, then the oregano. Add a good grinding of pepper.

4 Drizzle with the olive oil, then bake in the oven for about 20 minutes until cooked through and the cheese is melted, bubbling and turning lightly golden in just a few places.

5 Scatter with the parsley and serve.

Extra-special pizza napolitana

SERVES 1–2

1 frozen stone-baked Marguerita pizza

FOR THE TOPPING

50 g/2 oz/½ cup grated Mozzarella cheese

3 tomatoes, sliced

10 fresh basil leaves, torn

A good pinch of dried oregano

15 ml/1 tbsp olive oil

Freshly ground black pepper

1 black olive

1 Preheat the oven to 220°C/425°F/gas 7/fan oven 200°C. Put the pizza on a baking (cookie) sheet.

2 Scatter the Mozzarella over, then arrange the tomatoes on top. Sprinkle with half the basil and the oregano.

3 Drizzle the olive oil over and add a good grinding of pepper. Place the olive in the centre.

4 Bake in the oven for about 20 minutes until cooked through and the cheese is melted, bubbling and turning lightly golden in just a few places.

5 Scatter with the remaining basil and serve.

Naanwich

Naan breads make great snacks – especially with rich, nutritious toppings or fillings. Try them here wrapped around a version of thick dhal spiced with curry paste and sweetened with mango chutney. They make a great snack on their own, or a delicious side dish with a curry.

SERVES 4

2 large naan breads with garlic and coriander (cilantro)

1 x 225 g/8 oz/small can of pease pudding

10 ml/2 tsp curry paste

30 ml/2 tbsp mango chutney, chopped if necessary

Bottled lemon juice

4 handfuls of shredded lettuce

1 Grill (broil) or microwave the naans according to the packet directions.

2 Heat the pease pudding in a saucepan with the curry paste, stirring, or put in a bowl and microwave on High for about 1–2 minutes, stirring once, until piping hot.

3 Spread the pease pudding over the naans and spread the mango chutney over. Sprinkle with lemon juice and add the shredded lettuce.

4 Fold the naans into halves, then cut into wedges. Wrap in kitchen paper (paper towels) and eat with the fingers.

Naan vegetable pizza

Naan breads make ideal pizza bases too. Here they are topped with a piquant curry sauce and vegetables for a delicious snack meal. Experiment with other toppings such as cooked chicken, spicy sausages or even diced bought tandoori chicken. I like mango chutney on the side, but you could use other spicy pickles.

SERVES 4

4 plain naan breads

60 ml/4 tbsp mild curry paste

30 ml/2 tbsp tomato purée (paste)

60 ml/4 tbsp medium-fat soft cheese

½ x 350 g/12 oz packet of stir-fry vegetables with onions and peppers

100 g/4 oz/1 cup grated Cheddar cheese

TO SERVE
Mango chutney

1 Put the naans on two baking (cookie) sheets. Preheat the oven to 200°C/400°F/gas 6/fan oven 180°C.

2 Mix the curry paste with the tomato purée and the soft cheese. Spread over the naans. Scatter the vegetables over and sprinkle with the grated cheese.

3 Bake in the oven for 18–20 minutes until bubbling and cooked through.

4 Serve hot with mango chutney.

Nacho snack

This makes a gorgeous dish and you don't even need one of the trendy Tex-mex kits now available. Use less chilli powder if you don't like hot spicy food – there are hot and mild versions and you'll also find that the different brands vary in strength anyway. You'll soon get to know how much you like to add.

SERVES UP TO 8

1 x 425 g/15 oz/1 large can of red kidney beans, drained

10 ml/2 tsp dried minced onion

1.5 ml/¼ tsp chilli powder

15 ml/1 tbsp tomato purée (paste)

A good pinch of caster (superfine) sugar

Freshly ground black pepper

1 x 200 g/7 oz/large packet of corn tortilla chips

175 g/6 oz/1½ cups grated mild Cheddar cheese

1 Preheat the oven to 200°C/400°F/gas 6/fan oven 180°C. Mash the beans with a potato masher in a bowl. Work in the onion, chilli, tomato purée and sugar. Add a good grinding of pepper.

2 Spread a little of the mixture on each tortilla chip and lay them on a large baking (cookie) sheet, or use several individual shallow ovenproof dishes if you prefer.

3 Sprinkle liberally with the cheese and bake in the oven for about 8 minutes until the cheese is melted and is bubbling. Serve straight away.

desserts

The dessert is usually the pièce de résistance of any meal. But bought puddings always look and taste exactly that – bought – and making elegant ones from scratch takes time and effort. Here you have the perfect combination – absolutely divine, innovative desserts, beautifully put together, but with every possible corner cut for convenience.

Rum and chocolate cups

Smooth, rich chocolate mousse laced with rum, then spooned into chocolate cups
and served with slices of cool kiwi fruit – a superb dessert worthy of any dinner party.
This glorious pudding doesn't even have to have chocolate melted, it's just all mixed
up in no more than an instant! See photograph opposite page 120.

SERVES 6

**250 ml/8 fl oz/1 cup double
(heavy) cream**

**30 ml/2 tbsp dark Belgian
chocolate spread**

15 ml/1 tbsp rum

6 ready-made chocolate cup cases

1 small chocolate flake bar

2 or 3 kiwi fruit, sliced

**TO SERVE
Amaretti biscuits (cookies)**

1 Whip the cream until peaking. Spoon about a third of the cream into a separate bowl and reserve.

2 Fold the chocolate spread and rum into the remaining cream.

3 Spoon into the chocolate cases and level the tops. Spread or pipe the remaining cream on top of each cup. Chill until ready to serve.

4 Crumble the flake bar and scatter a little on top of each cup. Place on small plates with two or three slices of kiwi fruit arranged attractively to one side. Serve with amaretti biscuits.

Whisky cream liqueur crème caramel

I thoroughly recommend crème caramel mix in its own right – it really is remarkably good for a family meal or for a supper party. But, for a special occasion, this transforms a simple everyday pudding into a creamy, alcohol-laced sensation. You'll understand my enthusiasm once you've tried it!

SERVES 4

1 packet of crème caramel mix

Milk

75 ml/5 tbsp whisky cream liqueur

30 ml/2 tbsp icing (confectioners') sugar for dusting

60–90 ml/4–6 tbsp double (heavy) cream, to decorate

1 Make up the crème caramel mix according to the packet instructions but using 75 ml/5 tbsp less milk. Remove from the heat and stir in the liqueur.

2 Divide the contents of the caramel sachet between four ramekin dishes (custard cups). Pour the crème mixture carefully on top. Leave to cool, then chill.

3 When ready to serve, carefully loosen the edges and turn the crème caramels out on to four small serving plates. Dust the edges of the plates with sifted icing sugar and trickle a little cream round the crème caramels.

Cherry strudels

Making strudel dough is a long, complicated procedure and good results are not guaranteed. Admittedly, it can be fun, but it is always time-consuming. This recipe means no patient stretching and resting of dough and no stoning of fresh fruit – but the results are just divine.

SERVES 6

6 sheets of filo pastry (paste)

25 g/1 oz/2 tbsp butter, melted

1 x 410 g/14½ oz/large can of black cherry pie filling

1 trifle sponge, crumbled

30 ml/2 tbsp ground almonds

30 ml/2 tbsp icing (confectioners') sugar, sifted

150 ml/¼ pt/⅔ cup crème fraîche

30 ml/2 tbsp toasted flaked (slivered) almonds

1 Preheat the oven to 200°C/400°F/gas 6/fan oven 180°C. Lay a sheet of pastry on a work surface. Brush with melted butter, fold in half widthways and brush again.

2 Spoon a sixth of the pie filling along one edge, not quite to the ends.

3 Mix together the cake crumbs and ground almonds and sprinkle a sixth over.

4 Fold in the sides, then roll up, not too tightly. Brush a baking (cookie) sheet with a little of the remaining butter. Transfer the strudel to the sheet. Repeat with the remaining pastry sheets and filling. Brush the strudels with the remaining butter.

5 Bake in the oven for about 20 minutes until golden.

6 Transfer the strudels to six small serving plates and dust them with the sifted icing sugar. Put a spoonful of crème fraîche to one side of each and sprinkle with the almonds.

Custard tart

If you make an egg custard the traditional way, it can cause problems – but not this time! If you want the best, the richest, the creamiest custard tart, use a can! With the grated nutmeg on top, no one will be able to tell the difference. In fact, this could be better than home-made!

SERVES 4–6

1 x 20 cm/8 in ready-made shortcrust pastry case (pie shell)

2 eggs

150 ml/¼ pt/⅔ cup milk

1 x 425 g/15 oz/large can of custard

25 g/1 oz/2 tbsp caster (superfine) sugar

A little grated nutmeg

1 Preheat the oven to 190°C/375°F/gas 5/fan oven 170°C. Put the pastry case on an ovenproof plate.

2 Beat together the remaining ingredients except the nutmeg. Spoon into the case and dust a little nutmeg over the surface.

3 Bake in the oven for 40 minutes until set.

4 Serve warm or cold.

Lemon tart

When I first made a traditional French lemon tart, I couldn't believe how much grating, squeezing and fiddling about it needed and how long it took to cook. It tasted perfectly fine but I was exhausted! When I created this cheat, I tried it on some French friends and they thought I must have bought it at the local pâtisserie.

SERVES 4–6

1 x 20 cm/8 in ready-made shortcrust pastry case (pie shell)

1 x 350 g/12 oz jar of lemon curd

15 ml/1 tbsp bottled lemon juice

1 egg

Icing (confectioners') sugar for dusting

1 Preheat the oven to 180°C/350°F/gas 4/fan oven 160°C. Put the pastry case on an ovenproof plate.

2 Beat the lemon curd with the lemon juice and egg. Spoon into the pastry case.

3 Bake in the oven for about 40 minutes until set.

4 Leave to cool, then chill. Dust with a little sifted icing sugar before serving.

Easy french apple tart

Another classic dish that everyone loves but usually buys ready-made (when it will either be tiny or extremely expensive) as it is such a performance to make. Not any more! I can't prevent you having to prepare the fruit but that really is the only work. The rest is pure cheat!

SERVES 6

1 x 20 cm/8 in ready-made pastry case (pie shell)

100 g/4 oz/⅓ cup golden (light corn) syrup

1 large egg

5 ml/1 tsp bottled lemon juice

60 ml/4 tbsp double (heavy) cream

2 Granny Smith or other sharp eating (dessert) apples

15 g/½ oz/1 tbsp butter

Icing (confectioners') sugar for dusting

TO SERVE
Crème fraîche

1 Place the pastry case in a flan dish (pie pan).

2 Beat the syrup with the egg and lemon juice. Spoon 45 ml/3 tbsp into a small bowl and reserve. Whisk the cream into the remainder. Pour into the pastry case.

3 Peel, quarter, core and slice the apples. Arrange attractively in the pastry case.

4 Brush the remaining syrup and egg mixture over and dot with the butter.

5 Place the dish on a baking (cookie) sheet and bake in a preheated oven at 200°C/400°F/gas 6/fan oven 180°C for 30 minutes. Turn down the heat to 180°C/350°F/gas 4/fan oven 160°C and continue to cook for about 20 minutes until the apples are cooked through and the top is golden.

6 Dust the top with a little sifted icing sugar and serve warm or cold with crème fraîche.

No-wait summer puddings

I love summer pudding but, when I fancy it, I want to eat it more or less then and there; I don't want to have to leave it for a day to soak first! This version means you don't have to stew any fruit, you don't have to leave it for hours in the fridge and, because they are in individual dishes, even turning them out isn't essential.

SERVES 6

2 x 290 g/10½ oz/medium cans of mixed berry fruits

9 slices of white bread from a large loaf, crusts removed

Oil for greasing

A little icing (confectioners') sugar for dusting

TO SERVE

Crème fraîche

1 Drain the fruit, reserving the juice. Dip six of the slices of bread in the juice and press one into each of six lightly oiled ramekin dishes (custard cups). Trim level with the rim and use the trimmings to fill any gaps in the sides.

2 Spoon some of the remaining juice over the bread so it is completely soaked. Spoon the fruit into the dishes.

3 Cut the remaining bread slices in half, dip them in the juice, then lay on the tops so they are covered in soaked bread. Press down firmly with the back of a spoon. Chill if time, but this isn't essential. Reserve any remaining juice.

4 Loosen the edges with a round-bladed knife and turn the summer puddings out on to small plates. If any bread is still white, spoon a little extra juice over it to soak completely. Dust the edges of the plates with sifted icing sugar and serve with crème fraîche.

Crushed grapefruit and lemon chiffon

Canned grapefruit is an often-forgotten commodity that doesn't just have to be served for breakfast when fresh fruit isn't available. This bitter-sweet fluffy dessert tastes far more impressive than its ingredients might suggest and makes a deliciously refreshing conclusion to any meal.

SERVES 6

1 tablet of lemon jelly (jello)

1 x 410 g/14 oz/large can of grapefruit segments, drained, reserving the juice

2 egg whites

1 x 170 g/6 oz/small can of evaporated milk, thoroughly chilled

150 ml/¼ pt/⅔ cup crème fraîche or extra thick cream

15 ml/1 tbsp toasted mixed nuts

TO SERVE
Lemon thin biscuits (cookies)

1 Dissolve the jelly tablet in the grapefruit juice, either in a saucepan or in a bowl in the microwave.

2 Crush the grapefruit with a fork and add to the jelly. Chill until the consistency of egg white.

3 Whisk the egg whites until stiff, then the evaporated milk until thick and frothy.

4 Fold the evaporated milk, then the egg whites into the almost-set jelly mixture.

5 Spoon into tall glasses and spoon the crème fraîche or cream on top. Sprinkle with the nuts and chill until set.

6 Serve with lemon thin biscuits.

Pineapple mallow meringue

This simple but utterly delicious dessert is a glorious mixture of textures and flavours: fruity, cool, creamy, chewy and crunchy all in one! If you are serving it to round off a dinner party, you can easily prepare everything in advance, and then just stir in the meringue at the last minute.

SERVES 6

1 x 410 g/14 oz/large can of pineapple pieces, drained

100 g/4 oz white marshmallows

300 ml/¹⁄₂ pt/1¹⁄₄ cups double (heavy) cream

45 ml/3 tbsp kirsch

2 meringue nests, crushed

Angelica 'leaves', to decorate

1 Dry the pineapple on kitchen paper (paper towels). Reserve six pieces for decoration. Cut the remainder into smaller pieces with scissors, then cut up the marshmallows the same way.

2 Whip the cream with the kirsch until softly peaking. Fold in the pineapple pieces and marshmallows. Chill.

3 When ready to serve, fold in the crushed meringues and spoon into tall glasses. Decorate the tops with the reserved pineapple pieces and angelica leaves. Serve within 30 minutes of adding the meringues.

Apricot and almond crisp

This is definitely one of my favourite storecupboard standbys. The orange jelly really enhances the flavour of the apricots and the sweet, crisp buttery topping complements the fruit perfectly. I like to use fruit in natural juice rather than syrup as it is less cloying and has a fresher flavour.

SERVES 6

1 x 410 g/14 oz/large can of apricot halves

1 orange jelly (jello) tablet

200 ml/7 fl oz/scant 1 cup boiling water

150 ml/¼ pt/⅔ cup fromage frais

150 ml/¼ pt/⅔ cup double (heavy) cream

40 g/1½ oz/3 tbsp butter

50 g/2 oz/½ cup flaked (slivered) almonds

30 ml/2 tbsp golden (light corn) syrup

50 g/2 oz/1 cup cornflakes

1 Purée the apricots with their juice in a blender or food processor.

2 Dissolve the jelly tablet in the water. Stir in the apricot purée.

3 When cold but not set, whisk in the fromage frais. Spoon the mixture into six glasses or a large glass dish. Chill until set.

4 Whip the cream and spread over the surface.

5 Melt the butter in a small saucepan. Add the almonds and heat until lightly golden. Stir in the syrup and remove from the heat. Stir in the cornflakes until thoroughly blended. Leave to cool.

6 When cool but not completely cold, pile on to the cream and chill until ready to serve.

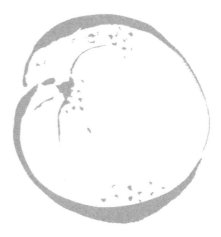

Strawberry butterscotch pancake layer

Yes, another marshmallow wonder! This time a stack of ready made pancakes is layered with fresh strawberries (you could use frozen or canned if you prefer) and cream and topped with a thick butterscotch sauce. It cuts beautifully so you don't have to worry when it comes to serving it up.

SERVES 6–8

50 g/2 oz white mini marshmallows (or large ones snipped with scissors)

50 g/2 oz/¼ cup unsalted (sweet) butter

45 ml/3 tbsp golden (light corn) syrup

15 ml/1 tbsp milk

10 ml/2 tsp bottled lemon juice

300 ml/½ pt/1¼ cups double (heavy) cream

30 ml/2 tbsp icing (confectioners') sugar

225 g/8 oz strawberries

1 packet of 6 sweet pancakes

1 Put the marshmallows, butter, syrup and milk in a saucepan and heat gently until melted and thoroughly blended. Remove from the heat, stir in the lemon juice, then stand the base of the pan in cold water to cool it quickly.

2 Whip the cream with the sugar until peaking. Reserve a few small strawberries for decoration. Hull and slice the remainder.

3 Put a pancake on a serving plate. Spread a fifth of the cream over, then scatter with a fifth of the strawberries. Repeat the layering, finishing with a pancake.

4 Spread the butterscotch sauce over the top so it trickles down the sides. Arrange the reserved strawberries attractively in the centre of the top.

5 Chill until ready to serve cut into wedges.

Rhubarb yoghurt mousse baskets

Nothing could be simpler than this dessert, yet it will look as if it took ages. Rhubarb and ginger are classic partners and this dish offers cool, fluffy rhubarb yoghurt mousse in crisp brandy snap baskets. Don't make the mousse more than two hours before you want to eat and don't fill the baskets until the last moment.

SERVES 6

2 egg whites

15 ml/1 tbsp caster (superfine) sugar

500 ml/17 fl oz/2¼ cups rhubarb and vanilla yoghurt

Icing (confectioners') sugar for dusting

6 ready-made brandy snap baskets

6 tiny sprigs of fresh mint

1 Whisk the egg whites until stiff. Whisk in the sugar until the mixture is standing in soft peaks. Fold in the yoghurt, then chill until ready to serve.

2 Dust six small serving plates with sifted icing sugar.

3 Spoon the mousse into the brandy snap baskets and place one on each plate. Decorate each with a tiny sprig of fresh mint and serve.

Triple chocolate baked alaska

I love this chocolate version of the traditional favourite. You can also make a strawberry Alaska by using strawberry ice-cream, plain meringue (increase the sugar by 50 g/2 oz/¼ cup and omit the chocolate powder) and spreading the base with strawberry jam or pie filling.

SERVES 6

1 x 15 cm/6 in sponge flan case (pie shell)

45 ml/3 tbsp chocolate hazelnut spread

3 egg whites

50 g/2 oz/½ cup drinking chocolate (sweetened chocolate) powder

100 g/4 oz/½ cup caster (superfine) sugar

8 scoops of chocolate ice-cream

6 glacé (candied) cherries and 6 angelica 'leaves', to decorate

1 Put the flan case on an ovenproof plate. Spread the chocolate hazelnut spread over the base.

2 Whisk the egg whites until stiff. Add the drinking chocolate powder and half the sugar and whisk until stiff and glossy. Fold in the remaining sugar.

3 Just before serving, preheat the oven to 230°C/450°F/gas 8/fan oven 210°C. Pile the scoops of ice-cream into the flan case and cover completely with the meringue so it stands in soft peaks. Decorate with the cherries and angelica leaves.

4 Bake immediately for 2 minutes until the meringue is turning golden in places. Serve immediately before the ice-cream melts.

Lemon and coconut pie

This dessert is as rich and delicious as a cheesecake but far easier to make – a no-bake crushed biscuit crumb case filled with ingredients you simply whisk together. Toasting the coconut gives it a nuttier flavour, but to keep it's texture don't put it on the filling until just before serving.

SERVES 6

1 x 225 g/8 oz packet of coconut ring biscuits (cookies)

100 g/4 oz/½ cup butter, melted

300 ml/½ pt/1¼ cups double (heavy) cream

1 x 350 g/12 oz/medium can of sweetened condensed milk

120 ml/4 fl oz/½ cup lemon juice

60 ml/4 tbsp desiccated (shredded) coconut

A small sprig of fresh mint, to decorate

1 Crush the biscuits and mix with the melted butter. Press into the base of a large flan dish (pie pan).

2 Lightly whip the cream, then gently whisk in the condensed milk and lemon juice.

3 When thickening, tip on to the biscuit base and level the surface. Chill overnight to set.

4 Toast the coconut in a dry frying pan (skillet) until lightly golden, stirring all the time. Tip out of the pan as soon as it is toasted to prevent over-browning. Leave to cool.

5 Just before serving, sprinkle the surface of the pie with the coconut and add a small sprig of fresh mint.

Peach and marron brulée

White peaches look fantastic, but they are usually only available whole or halved, so you'd have to slice them! Instead of caramelising the sugar with a blow torch or under the grill, you can use an extra 50 g/2 oz/¼ cup of sugar and melt it in a pan until golden, then pour it quickly over the chestnut mixture and leave to set.

SERVES 4

30 ml/2 tbsp cognac or brandy

1 x 225 g/8 oz/medium can of sweetened chestnut purée

250 ml/8 fl oz/1 cup crème fraîche

1 x 880 g/2 lb/very large can of peach slices, drained

About 100 g/4 oz/½ cup caster (superfine) sugar

1 Beat the cognac or brandy with the chestnut purée and the crème fraîche.

2 Slice the peaches and arrange in a shallow flameproof serving dish. Spoon the chestnut mixture over and chill for 30 minutes.

3 Sprinkle liberally with the sugar to cover the top completely. Either caramelise with a blow torch or place the dish under a preheated grill (broiler) until golden and bubbling.

4 Chill again until ready to serve.

Photograph opposite:
Rum and chocolate cups
(see page 106)

Ratafia and cointreau ice-cream

You may have thought that making ice-cream was a complicated business. This is just sweetened cream flavoured with orange liqueur, then mixed with crushed ratafias and frozen. The result is sublime! Plus it has the added advantage that you can prepare it in advance and it slices straight from the freezer.

SERVES 6–8

Sunflower oil for greasing

100 g/4 oz ratafias, plus a few for serving

600 ml/1 pt/2½ cups double (heavy) or whipping cream

50 g/2 oz/⅓ cup icing (confectioners') sugar

A pinch of salt

75 ml/5 tbsp Cointreau or other orange liqueur

6–8 fresh physalis (optional)

1 Oil a 900 g/2 lb loaf tin (pan) and line with clingfilm (plastic wrap) so it hangs over the edges all round. Brush thoroughly with oil. Put the ratafias in a plastic or paper bag and finely crush with a rolling pin. Coat the base and half way up the sides of the tin with half the crushed ratafias.

2 Whip the cream with the sugar and salt until softly peaking. Whisk in half the ratafias and the liqueur until standing in soft peaks again.

3 Turn the mixture into the prepared tin, level the surface, then gently fold the clingfilm over. Wrap the tin completely in foil and freeze until firm.

4 Just before serving, unwrap the tin and unfold the clingfilm over the surface so it is tucked back against the sides of the tin. Dip the tin briefly in hot water, then invert on to a serving plate. Hold the plate and tin firmly and give it a good shake to loosen the ice-cream. Lift away the tin and gently peel off the clingfilm.

5 Decorate the plate with a few whole ratafias and fresh physalis, if liked. Simply peel back the papery covers to reveal the orange fruit, and lay them on the plate in a cluster. Serve the ice-cream cut into slices.

Photograph opposite:
All-in-one carrot cake with cream cheese frosting (see page 131)

cakes and bakes

You can always buy cakes, breads and biscuits, of course, but there are times when you want to make something at home. However, starting from scratch is a time-consuming business so if you can cheat a bit then so much the better! Here you'll find everything from quick breads to gorgeous gateaux; all take the minimum of time to prepare and all taste and look superb.

Crisp seeded fingers

So you forgot to buy special bread for your dinner party? Don't panic! You can make these crisp buttery strips flavoured with seeds of your choice instead. All you need is a couple of storecupboard essentials and few standard loaf slices – they don't even have to be that fresh!

MAKES 18

6 slices of bread from a sliced loaf

Butter or margarine

Celery, fennel, caraway or poppy seeds

1 Preheat the oven to 190°C/375°F/gas 5/fan oven 170°C. Spread the bread slices on both sides with butter or margarine and sprinkle with the seeds. Cut each slice into three fingers.

2 Lay the fingers on a baking (cookie) sheet. Bake in the oven for about 15–20 minutes until golden and crisp.

3 Leave to cool on kitchen paper (paper towels).

Garlic croûtes

These can be stored in an airtight container for days. They are ideal to serve on their own as a crisp accompaniment to soups or starters, or can be topped with pâté, chopped egg, cheese or tapenade for nibbles. You can make your own garlic croûtons too, by simply dicing the slices before baking.

MAKES ABOUT 12

1 ready-to-bake garlic baguette

1 Preheat the oven to 190°C/370°F/gas 5/fan oven 170°C.

2 Cut the bread right through the slices and place a little apart on a baking (cookie) sheet. Bake in the oven for about 15–20 minutes until crisp and golden.

3 Cool on a wire rack. Store in an airtight container.

Fast-to-make cheese straws

I know you can buy these ready-made but the majority are usually broken in the packet and, anyway, everybody knows they're bought. These take just a few minutes to prepare, look and taste exceptionally good and will all be whole at serving time. You can use ready-grated Cheddar cheese instead of Parmesan if you prefer.

MAKES ABOUT 40

225 g/8 oz/2 cups plain (all-purpose) flour

100 g/4 oz/1 cup grated Parmesan cheese

1.5 ml/¼ tsp English mustard

A good pinch of salt

Freshly ground black pepper

90 ml/6 tbsp sunflower oil

60 ml/4 tbsp water

1 Grease a large baking (cookie) sheet. Preheat the oven to 190°C/375°F/gas 5/fan oven 170°C.

2 Put all the ingredients in a bowl and mix together with a fork – or pop them in a food processor and run the machine until the mixture forms a ball.

3 Roll out to about 10 cm/4 in wide and to a thickness of about 5 mm/¼ in. Cut into fingers and transfer to the baking sheet.

4 Bake in the oven for 15–20 minutes until straw coloured.

5 Allow to cool slightly, then transfer to a wire rack to cool completely.

6 Store in an airtight container.

Savoury sesame puffs

*Another version of bought savoury sticks – but much better. These have a
wonderfully intense sesame seed flavour because of the addition of tahini paste and
the results look and taste brilliant. I always keep a couple of packets of puff pastry in
the freezer because it's so versatile.*

MAKES ABOUT 32

**1 sheet of ready-rolled frozen puff
pastry (paste), thawed**

15 ml/1 tbsp tahini paste from a jar

1 egg, beaten

30 ml/2 tbsp sesame seeds

5 ml/1 tsp coarse sea salt

1 Dampen a baking (cookie) sheet. Preheat the oven to 200°C/400°F/
gas 6/fan oven 180°C.

2 Lay the pastry on a board. Stir the tahini paste well in the jar to mix
the oil into it. Take out a tablespoonful and spread it very thinly over
half the pastry. Fold over the other side of the pastry to form a
sandwich. Roll gently to stick the two halves together.

3 Brush the top with beaten egg, then sprinkle with the sesame seeds.
Roll gently again to stick the seeds to the surface, then sprinkle with
the sea salt. Cut into fairly thin sticks.

4 Transfer to the baking sheet and bake in the oven for 20 minutes
until crisp, golden and puffy.

5 Allow to cool slightly, then transfer to a wire rack to cool completely.

6 Store in an airtight container.

Marmite whirls

Savoury pinwheels of salty but flaky perfection are ideal to impress your guests before dinner. They can be made ages in advance because they keep well in an airtight container. Try preparing and baking them when you're already using the oven for another meal, just so they're ready when needed.

MAKES ABOUT 30

1 sheet of ready-rolled frozen puff pastry (paste), thawed

30 ml/2 tbsp Marmite or other yeast extract

50 g/2 oz/½ cup finely grated or crumbled mild cheese such as Cheshire

10 ml/2 tsp snipped chives

1 egg, beaten

1 Dampen a baking (cookie) sheet. Preheat the oven to 200°C/400°F/gas 6/fan oven 180°C.

2 Place the pastry on a board. Spread with the Marmite, then sprinkle with the cheese and chives. Roll up, starting at a short end. Cut into slices and lay them on the baking sheet. Brush with beaten egg to glaze.

3 Bake in the oven for 10–15 minutes until golden and puffy.

4 Transfer to a wire rack to cool.

5 Store in an airtight container.

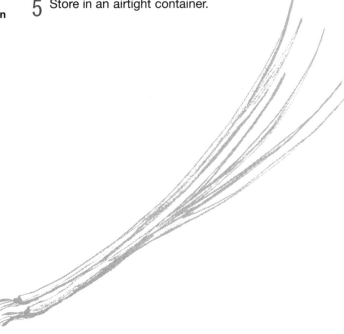

Melba toast

Purists say that to make melba toast you must first toast the bread on both sides, then cut it in half through the middle, then bake it. This way takes out all that hassle and the results are just as good. Again, you can buy melba toast but it doesn't look the same as 'the real thing'!

MAKES 12 PIECES

12 slices of white bread from a small cut loaf

1 Preheat the oven to 150°C/300°F/gas 2/fan oven 135°C. Stack the bread in a pile and cut off the crusts (save these to use for breadcrumbs).

2 Roll the slices one at a time with a rolling pin to flatten. Place on one or two baking (cookie) sheets.

3 Bake in the oven for about 30 minutes or until pale golden and curling at the edges.

4 Cool on a wire rack.

5 Store in an airtight container.

Quick white loaf

This isn't exactly a cheat but I wanted to include it because there's no arm-aching kneading or prolonged rising periods and it's the ideal storecupboard standby for when you run out of white bread. You can shape the dough into rolls, too, if you prefer, and they'll only take about 12–15 minutes to cook.

MAKES 1 LOAF

450 g/1 lb/4 cups self-raising (self-rising) flour, plus extra for dusting

10 ml/2 tsp baking powder

5 ml/1 tsp salt

5 ml/1 tsp caster (superfine) sugar

25 g/1 oz/2 tbsp soft tub margarine

5 ml/1 tsp bottled lemon juice

300 ml/½ pt/1¼ cups milk

1 Preheat the oven to 220°C/425°F/gas 7/fan oven 200°C. Grease a baking (cookie) sheet. Mix together the flour, baking powder, salt and sugar.

2 Add the margarine and mash it into the flour with a fork, working it against the sides of the bowl until the mixture looks crumbly.

3 Add the lemon juice and enough milk to form a soft but not sticky dough.

4 Shape the dough into a ball and place on the baking sheet. Mark a cross in the top with a knife. Dust with a little flour.

5 Bake in the oven for 20–25 minutes until golden, risen and the base sounds hollow when tapped.

6 Cool on a wire rack.

No-knead wholemeal loaf

This is another version of a perfectly tasty no-effort bread, ideal when you've only got stale crusts left in the breadbin and everyone wants bread and cheese for lunch! It can be made and baked within half an hour and has a lovely texture and flavour. It's best eaten fresh when just cooled, or sliced and toasted.

MAKES 1 LOAF

450 g/1 lb/4 cups self-raising (self-rising) wholemeal flour, plus extra for dusting

10 ml/2 tsp baking powder

5 ml/1 tsp salt

30 ml/2 tbsp sunflower or olive oil

10 ml/2 tsp clear honey

5 ml/1 tsp bottled lemon juice

350 ml/12 fl oz/1⅓ cups milk, plus extra for glazing

5 ml/1 tsp poppy or sunflower seeds

1 Preheat the oven to 220°C/425°F/gas 7/fan oven 200°C. Grease a baking (cookie) sheet. Mix together the flour, baking powder and salt.

2 Add the oil, honey and lemon juice and stir in. Then mix with enough milk to form a soft but not sticky dough.

3 Shape the dough into a ball and place on the baking sheet. Mark a cross in the top with a knife. Brush with a little milk and sprinkle with the seeds.

4 Bake in the oven for about 25 minutes until golden, risen and the base sounds hollow when tapped.

5 Cool on a wire rack.

Triple chocolate fudge cake

I find bought sponge cake mixes taste rather synthetic if they are made according to the instructions. However, this recipe transforms a simple mix into a moist, sinful cake – richer and more chocolatey than any you could buy – and it takes hardly any effort to make. So go on, indulge yourself!

MAKES ONE 18 CM/7 IN CAKE

1 chocolate sponge mix

60 ml/4 tbsp chocolate spread

1 large egg

Water

1 Mars Bar

30 ml/2 tbsp cocoa (unsweetened chocolate) powder

50 g/2 oz/¼ cup butter or margarine

175 g/6 oz/1 cup icing (confectioners') sugar, sifted

30 ml/2 tbsp milk

1 Preheat the oven to 200°C/400°F/gas 6/fan oven 180°C. Grease and line the bases of two 18 cm/7 in sandwich tins (pans) with greased greaseproof (waxed) paper.

2 Empty the cake mix into a bowl. Add 30 ml/2 tbsp of the chocolate spread, the egg and the quantity of water as stated on the packet. Beat for 2 minutes. Add the remaining water as stated and beat for a further 1 minute.

3 Divide the mixture between the tins and level the surfaces. Bake in the oven for about 15 minutes until risen and the centres spring back when lightly pressed.

4 Allow to cool slightly, then turn out on to a wire rack to cool completely.

5 Break up the Mars Bar and melt with the remaining chocolate spread, the cocoa and the butter or margarine in a saucepan (or in a bowl in the microwave), stirring frequently.

6 Gradually beat in the icing sugar and the milk until the mixture forms stiff peaks.

7 Use some of the mixture to sandwich the cake together on a serving plate, then spread the remainder all over the outside, dipping the knife in hot water for easy spreading.

All-in-one carrot cake with cream cheese frosting

This is the moistest, most delicious carrot cake I have ever made and it takes the least time to prepare! You can use a low-fat soft cheese for the frosting instead of cream cheese but you'll need more icing sugar as it is not as firm. Just keep adding a little at a time until you reach the right consistency. See photograph opposite page 121.

MAKES ONE 900 G/2 LB CAKE

FOR THE CAKE

175 g/6 oz/³/₄ cup soft tub margarine

175 g/6 oz/³/₄ cup light brown sugar

250 g/9 oz/2¹/₄ cups self-raising (self-rising) flour

5 ml/1 tsp baking powder

2 large eggs

300 g/11 oz/1 medium can of carrots, drained

5 ml/1 tsp vanilla essence (extract)

2.5 ml/¹/₂ tsp mixed (apple pie) spice

50 g/2 oz/¹/₂ cup chopped walnuts (optional)

FOR THE FROSTING

25 g/1 oz/2 tbsp cream cheese

100 g/4 oz/²/₃ cup icing (confectioners') sugar, sifted

Bottled lemon juice

1 Put all the cake ingredients in a bowl and beat with a wooden spoon until well blended (or do this in a mixer or food processor).

2 Preheat the oven to 180°C/350°F/gas 4/fan oven 160°C. Grease a 900 g/2 lb loaf tin (pan) and line the base with non-stick baking parchment or greased greaseproof (waxed) paper.

3 Turn the mixture into the tin and level the surface. Bake in the oven for about 1 hour until risen, golden and the centre springs back when lightly pressed.

4 Allow to cool slightly, then turn out on to a wire rack, remove the paper and leave to cool completely.

5 Beat the cream cheese with the icing sugar and sharpen with lemon juice to taste. Spread over the top of the cake, allowing it to trickle down the sides, then leave it to set.

Chocolate flake squares

When friends are popping in and you need something sweet to give them, a plain packet of digestives biscuits might not be enough. This no-bake chocolate and biscuit concoction is mouthwateringly ideal. It's also great served for dessert with whipped cream or crème fraîche.

MAKES ABOUT 30

1 x 225 g/8 oz packet of digestive biscuits (graham crackers)

50 g/2 oz/¼ cup light brown sugar

45 ml/3 tbsp golden (light corn) syrup

100 g/4 oz/½ cup butter or hard block margarine

75 ml/5 tbsp cocoa (unsweetened chocolate) powder

5 ml/1 tsp vanilla essence (extract)

100 g/4 oz/⅔ cup icing (confectioners') sugar

15 ml/1 tbsp water

1 large chocolate flake bar, crushed

1 Grease an 18 x 28 cm/7 x 11 in shallow baking tin (pan). Roughly crush the biscuits (cookies) but leave them in small pieces, not crumbs.

2 Melt together the sugar, syrup, butter or margarine, 45 ml/3 tbsp of the cocoa and the vanilla in a saucepan, stirring. Bring to the boil and remove from the heat.

3 Stir in the biscuit pieces and press the mixture into the prepared tin.

4 Sift the remaining cocoa with the icing sugar and mix with the water to form a thick cream, adding a few drops more water if necessary. Spread over the surface of the biscuit mixture, sprinkle with the crushed flake and leave to set.

5 Cut into small squares for serving.

Chocolate oat crunchy bars

These are so expensive to buy but take hardly any time at all to make. You can ring the changes by adding hazelnuts, almonds, sunflower or pumpkin seeds, chocolate chips or other dried fruits, such as chopped apricots, peaches, pears, apples or prunes instead of the raisins.

MAKES 12–16

175 g/6 oz/¾ cup butter or hard block margarine

50 g/2 oz/¼ cup light brown sugar

30 ml/2 tbsp golden (light corn) syrup

5 ml/1 tsp vanilla essence (extract)

75 g/3 oz/½ cup raisins

350 g/12 oz/3 cups crunchy oat and fruit cereal

225 g/8 oz/2 cups plain (semi-sweet) or milk (sweet) chocolate

1 Oil or dampen an 18 x 28 cm/7 x 11 in shallow baking tin (pan) and line with non-stick baking parchment.

2 Melt the butter or margarine, sugar and syrup in a pan. Stir in the vanilla, raisins and cereal.

3 Turn into the prepared tin and press right out to the corners.

4 Break up the chocolate in a small bowl and either melt in a pan of hot water or heat briefly in the microwave. Spread over the surface of the oat mixture to cover completely.

5 Chill until firm, then cut into fingers or squares and store in an airtight container.

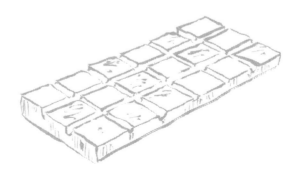

simple sauces

When you want a basic sauce, it's much better to make it yourself than to buy a packet. But they can often be rather complicated. Here are the best cheats I know for excellent results with the minimum of fuss. They all use basic ingredients you'll already have in your kitchen so are worth having in your repertoire.

Béchamel sauce

This sauce usually requires you to infuse the milk with onion, herbs and spices first, then make a roux (a blend of butter and flour), then cook them carefully together to create the finished sauce. I find this one-step method tastes just as good even though it's much easier and far less likely to go lumpy.

SERVES 4

20 g/³⁄₄ oz/3 tbsp plain (all-purpose) flour

300 ml/¹⁄₂ pt/1¹⁄₄ cups milk

A good knob of butter or margarine

1 bouquet garni sachet

Onion salt

Freshly ground black pepper

1 Put the flour in a small saucepan. Gradually whisk in the milk with a wire whisk.

2 Add the butter or margarine and bouquet garni sachet. Bring to the boil and boil for 2 minutes, whisking all the time, until thick and smooth.

3 Press the bouquet garni sachet against the side of the pan to extract as much flavour as possible. Season the sauce to taste with onion salt and pepper and use as required.

VARIATIONS

Cheese sauce
Add 2.5 ml/¹⁄₂ tsp Dijon or English mustard and a good handful of grated Cheddar or blue cheese to the cooked sauce and heat gently, stirring, until melted.

Parsley sauce
Add a good handful of chopped fresh or frozen parsley to the cooked sauce.

Hollandaise sauce

Traditionally, this sauce uses egg yolks only and you have to whisk it for ages in a bowl over a pan of hot water. Not only is it annoying to have extra whites left over, using the whole egg makes the sauce much less temperamental so you can cook it in a saucepan as long as you keep the heat low.

SERVES 4

2 eggs

30 ml/2 tbsp bottled lemon juice

100 g/4 oz/½ cup butter, melted

A pinch of cayenne

Salt and freshly ground black pepper

1 Whisk the eggs and lemon juice in a saucepan. Gradually whisk in the melted butter a little at a time.

2 Cook over a very gentle heat, whisking all the time, until thick. Don't allow it to boil or the mixture will curdle. Remove from the heat as soon as it has thickened.

3 Season to taste with the cayenne, salt and pepper.

Smooth tomato sauce

This brilliant basic sauce has so many uses. It is lovely served with ravioli or other stuffed pasta or as a pouring sauce with grilled or fried meats, poultry or fish. For added flavour, use passata with basil or garlic, or add a few extra chopped fresh herbs to the sauce. A touch of sugar just brings out the flavour of the tomatoes.

SERVES 4

15 ml/1 tbsp cornflour (cornstarch)

30 ml/2 tbsp water

300 ml/½ pt/1¼ cup passata (sieved tomatoes)

A good pinch of caster (superfine) sugar

Salt and freshly ground black pepper

1 Blend the cornflour with the water in a small saucepan.

2 Add the passata and heat, stirring all the time, until thickened and bubbling. Boil for 1 minute, stirring.

3 Season to taste with the sugar, salt and pepper.

Chunky tomato sauce

You can chop an onion and fry it gently in a little olive oil for 2 minutes until soft but not brown instead of using the dried onion if you like – it just means a bit more effort. If serving the sauce, made as below, with pasta, add a tablespoonful of olive oil when you start simmering it.

15 ml/1 tbsp dried minced onion

1 x 400 g/14 oz/large can of chopped tomatoes

15 ml/1 tbsp tomato purée (paste)

1 large garlic clove, crushed, or 5 ml/1 tsp garlic purée (optional)

2.5 ml/½ tsp dried mixed herbs, basil or oregano

2.5 ml/½ tsp caster (superfine) sugar

Salt and freshly ground black pepper

1 Put all the ingredients in a saucepan.

2 Bring to the boil, reduce the heat and simmer gently for 4–5 minutes until pulpy. Use as required.

Storecupboard barbecue sauce

You can use bottled table barbecue sauce for both basting food and serving with it but, if you haven't any, you can make a superb one with everyday ingredients that need no cooking. If you do use the lovely ground red Spanish pimentón pepper, it gives a superb smoky flavour to the sauce.

SERVES 4

30 ml/2 tbsp tomato ketchup (catsup)

30 ml/2 tbsp golden (light corn) syrup

30 ml/2 tbsp any vinegar

15 ml/1 tbsp Worcestershire sauce

2.5 ml/½ tsp pimentón (optional)

2.5 ml/½ tsp garlic granules (optional)

1 Whisk together all the ingredients. Use as a base or dip.

2 Store any remainder in a screw-topped jar in the cupboard.

Gooey butterscotch sauce

Marshmallows are one of the most versatile of sweet storecupboard ingredients – they make a sauce that's gooey, velvety and almost unctuous! If you can only buy large marshmallows, snip them into smaller pieces using wet scissors – that way they don't stick to the blades.

SERVES 4

A good handful of mini marshmallows

A good knob of butter

90 ml/6 tbsp milk

30 ml/2 tbsp golden (light corn) syrup

Bottled lemon juice

1 Place all the ingredients except the lemon juice in a saucepan.

2 Heat gently, stirring all the time, until melted, smooth and gooey. Sharpen to taste with a dash of lemon juice.

Instant chocolate sauce

You can, obviously, make as little or as much as you like of this sauce. The quantities here make a generous amount for one person. Serve it over ice-cream or with fruit (particularly bananas or pears). Make sure you use a chocolate powder that you make into a drink just by adding water, not milk.

SERVES 1

45 ml/3 tbsp instant drinking (sweetened) chocolate powder

Boiling water

1 Put the powder in a small bowl. Using a wire whisk, work in boiling water, 5 ml/1 tsp at a time, to form a thick paste. Then stir in a little more to form a smooth pouring sauce.

Hot sinful chocolate sauce

This may not be original but it is one of the best sauces around. It was first created using Mars bars but I find loads of other chocolate bars make heavenly sauces – my particular favourite is using one with a runny caramel centre. If you want to experiment to find you own favourite, I can't think of a better excuse!

SERVES 2–4

1 standard-sized Mars, fudge or other filled chocolate bar

75–90 ml/5–6 tbsp milk

A knob of butter or margarine

1 Break up the chocolate bar and place in a saucepan.

2 Add the milk and butter or margarine. Heat, stirring all the time, until melted, thick and smooth. Serve hot.

Index